# AIRCRAFT
# CORROSION CONTROL

International Standard Book Number 0-89100-111-5
For sale by: IAP, Inc., A Hawks Industries Company
Mail To: P.O. Box 10000, Casper, WY 82602-1000
Ship To: 7383 6WN Road, Casper, WY 82604-1835
(800) 443-9250 ❖ (307) 266-3838 ❖ FAX: (307) 472-5106
HBC1094    Printed in the USA

IAP, Inc.; 7383 6WN Road, Casper, WY 82604-1835

Printed in the United States of America

Library of Congress Cataloging-in-publication number: 93-30064

# Contents

# Preface

This book on *Aircraft Corrosion Control* is one of a series of specialized training manuals prepared for aviation maintenance personnel.

This series is part of a programmed learning course developed and produced by IAP, one of the largest suppliers of aviation maintenance training materials in the world. This program is part of a continuing effort to improve the quality of education for aviation mechanics throughout the world.

The purpose of each IAP training series is to provide basic information on the operation and principles of the various aircraft systems and their components. Specific information on detailed operation procedures should be obtained from the manufacturer through his appropriate maintenance manuals, and followed in detail for the best results.

This particular manual on *Aircraft Corrosion Control* includes a series of carefully prepared questions and answers to emphasize key elements of the study,

and to encourage you to continually test yourself for accuracy and retention as you use this book. A multiple choice final examination is included to allow you to test your comprehension of the total material.

Some of the words may be new to you. They are defined in the Glossary found at the back of the book.

The validity of any program such as this is enhanced immeasurably by the cooperation shown IAP by recognized experts in the field, and by the willingness of the various manufacturers to share their literature and answer countless questions in the preparation of these programs.

If you have any questions or comments regarding this manual, or any of the many other textbooks offered by IAP, simply contact: Sales Department, IAP Inc.; Mailing Address: P.O. Box 10000, Casper, WY 82602-1000; Shipping Address: 7383 6WN Road, Casper, WY 82604-1835; or call toll free: (800) 443-9250; International, call: (307) 266-3838.

# Introduction

Modern aircraft are made of lightweight metals which are highly reactive to contaminants in the atmosphere. Salt air from coastal regions and industrial contaminants from urban areas attack aluminum alloy and magnesium structures and, according to an estimate made by the Air Transport Association, cost the American industry some six billion dollars a year for damage due to corrosion.

Corrosion is a complex electro-chemical action that causes metals to be transformed into their salts and oxides. These powdery substances replace the metal and cause severe loss of strength in the structure. While complex in its nature, the actual mechanics of corrosion are relatively simple and straight forward. For corrosion to form, three requirements must be met:

1. There must be an electrical potential difference within the metal.
2. There must be a conductive path between the two areas of potential difference.
3. There must be some form of electrolyte or fluid covering the two areas.

Corrosion is a natural process, and its prevention is almost impossible; but it can be controlled. The aviation technician must prevent or remove one or more of the requirements for corrosion. In doing this, he goes a long way in adding longevity to the structure of the airplane.

Cleanliness of the surface is one of the best ways to control corrosion. When moisture is held in contact with the metal surface by an accumulation of dirt or grease, corrosion is sure to start. If the surface can be kept perfectly dry and clean, however, corrosion has little chance of getting started. The essence of corrosion control is therefore prevention rather than removal.

Once corrosion has formed, all the technician can do is to remove every trace of the corrosion products, treat the surface to form a protective, non porous oxide film, and restore the protective and decorative finish. If the damage is too extensive, all that can be done is replacement of the affected skin or component.

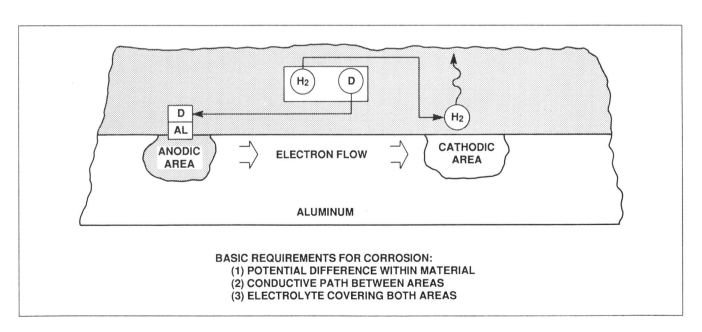

BASIC REQUIREMENTS FOR CORROSION:
(1) POTENTIAL DIFFERENCE WITHIN MATERIAL
(2) CONDUCTIVE PATH BETWEEN AREAS
(3) ELECTROLYTE COVERING BOTH AREAS

# Chapter I

# Understanding Corrosion

In order to understand corrosion, we must understand the basic facts of electro-chemistry. For this is what corrosion is — electro-chemical action.

All matter is made up of atoms and molecules. An atom is the basic unit of a chemical element, while a molecule is a cluster of atoms which make up the smallest identifiable unit of a chemical compound. For example, sodium (Na) is a metallic element and consists simply of atoms. Combined with chlorine (Cl), however, it forms a molecule of sodium chloride — (NaCl) common table salt.

An atom consists of a nucleus made up of protons having positive charges and neutrons with no charge. Surrounding the nucleus are electrons, negatively charged particles of electrical energy. If the atom has exactly the same number of electrons as protons, it is considered to be balanced. If there are more or less electrons than protons, the atom is said to be charged. This charged atom is called an ion. If there are more electrons than protons, it is a negative ion. If there are more protons than electrons, it is a positive ion. An ion is unstable, always seeking to lose or gain the extra electrons which will change it back into a balanced or neutral atom.

Electrons are the particles of electrical energy that flow, or move in circuits, and it is the movement of these sub-microscopic charges with which we are concerned.

Metals may be arranged in a table known as the Electro-Chemical Series, Figure 1-1, showing the relative ease with which these metals ionize. The earlier the metal appears in the series, the more active it is; or, as we will see later, the more anodic it will act in the formation of corrosion. Many metals will become ionized due to galvanic action when brought into contact with even dilute acids, salts, or alkalis such as are found in industrially contaminated air. If an aluminum structure is in contact with moisture having a trace of hydrochloric acid, there will be a chemical reaction between the acid and the aluminum to form aluminum chloride and hydrogen.

$$2Al + 6HCl - 2AlCl_3 + 3H_2$$

The hydrogen is released as a gas, and the salt, aluminum chloride, forms a white powder on the surface; this is the visible evidence of corrosion.

Corrosion is an electro-chemical action in which a metal is changed into a chemical salt; or, as we sometimes think of it, is eaten away. When two metals are in contact with each other and in the presence of an electrolyte such as hydrochloric acid, the less active metal acts as a cathode, attracting electrons from the anode, which is thus subject to corrosion. Perhaps the easiest way to visualize what is actually taking place is to consider a very simple battery, Figure 1-2. If we take any two separate metals and immerse them in an acid, salt, or alkaline solution, acting as the electrolyte, a battery is formed. This battery produces a flow of electrons between the two metals as long as:

1. the metals exist.

2. the solution remains acidic, salt or alkaline.

3. a conductive path connects the two metals.

In this example, we put a piece of copper and a piece of aluminum in a weak solution of hydrochloric acid. In the electro-chemical series, aluminum is

```
ARRANGED IN ORDER OF ELECTRODE POTENTIAL (NOBILITY).
MOST ANODIC—WILL GIVE UP ELECTRONS MOST EASILY.

MAGNESIUM
ZINC
CLAD 7075 ALUMINUM ALLOY
COMMERCIALLY PURE ALUMINUM (1100)
CLAD 2024 ALUMINUM ALLOY
CADMIUM
7075-T6 ALUMINUM ALLOY
2024-T3 ALUMINUM ALLOY
MILD STEEL
LEAD
TIN
COPPER
STAINLESS STEEL
SILVER
NICKEL
CHROMIUM
GOLD
MOST CATHODIC—LEAST CORROSIVE.

ANY METAL APPEARING BEFORE ANOTHER IN THIS
SERIES IS ANODIC TO ANY METAL WHICH FOLLOWS
IT, AND WILL BE THE ONE CORRODED WHEN THEY
ARE SUBJECT TO GALVANIC ACTION.
```

Figure 1-1. Electro-chemical series for metals.

considerably more active than copper. When electrons flow from the aluminum through the conductor to the copper, positive aluminum ions are left. Two of these ions attract six negative chlorine atoms from the acid and form two molecules of aluminum chloride, $AlCl_3$, on the surface of the aluminum. This eats away some of the base metal. The six positive hydrogen ions left in the acid are attracted to the copper by the electrons which came from the aluminum. The hydrogen ions are neutralized, form three hydrogen molecules ($H_2$), and leave the surface as free hydrogen gas.

One of the basic characteristics of metals is their electrode potential. This simply means that when two dissimilar metals are placed in an electrolyte, there will exist between these two metals an electrical potential or voltage. This force will cause the electrons in the more negative material to flow to the less negative material — the cathode — if a conductive path is provided.

In Figure 1-3, we have a piece of aluminum alloy such as 2024, of which most aircraft structure is made. Copper is the chief alloying agent. The microscopic grains of the material serve as the anode and cathode for our explanation. Aluminum is more negative than copper and will form the anode of the

galvanic action that takes place. Within the metal itself, the forces are such that there will be no flow of electrons between the two alloying agents until an external path is provided to form a complete circuit. The path, the electrolyte, may be a film of moisture on the surface containing pollutants such as acid, salt, or other industrial contaminants. In our illustration we will stick with a little hydrochloric acid in the atmosphere.

The electrode potential difference between the aluminum and the copper grains causes positive ions to exist within the aluminum. When an electrolyte film covers the surface, the aluminum ions attract chlorine ions from the hydrochloric acid and form aluminum chloride, the salt of corrosion. Hydrogen ions will be attracted to the copper by the electrons from the aluminum. These hydrogen ions will be neutralized and form molecules ($H_2$) which leave the surface as a free gas. Corrosion has formed on the aluminum, the anode. No corrosion products are evident on the copper, the cathode.

This type of electro-chemical attack produces pits of corrosion salts, and is usually rather localized. If, on the other hand, the entire surface is covered with a strong electrolyte, there will be so much corrosion that it will produce a more or less uniformly damaged

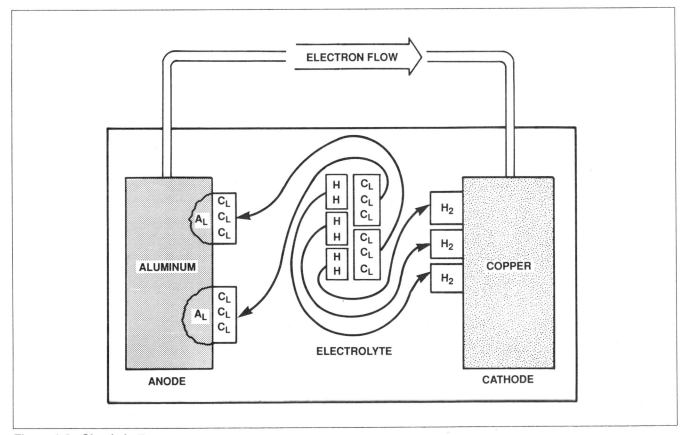

*Figure 1-2. Simple battery.*

2

area. This type of corrosion is called a direct chemical attack.

From this basic introduction, we see three requirements for its formation:

1. There must be areas of unequal electrode potential.
2. There must be a conductive path through the metal between these areas.

3. On the surface between these areas, there must be a conductive, chemical path containing materials to unite with the metal to form chemical salts.

Corrosion control by the A&P technician consists of preventing this chemical action by eliminating one or more of these three basic requirements.

# Study Questions:

1. What is the difference between an atom and a molecule?

2. What is an ion?

3. What is the white powder which forms on the surface of aluminum when it corrodes?

4. What actually happens to a metal when it corrodes?

5. What is meant by electrode potential difference within a metal?

6. What is the chief alloying agent in 2024 aluminum alloy?

7. In an aluminum and copper alloy, which metal will be eaten away by corrosion?

8. What are the three basic requirements for the formation of corrosion?

9. What steps can a technician take to minimize damage from corrosion?

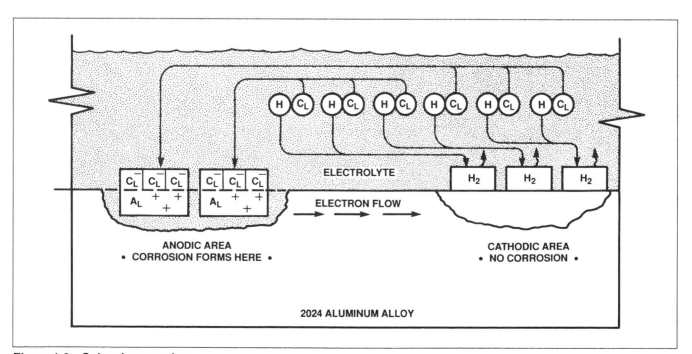

*Figure 1-3. Galvanic corrosion.*

# Chapter II

# Classifying Corrosion

## A. Oxidation

One of the more simple forms of corrosion, and perhaps the one with which we are most familiar, dry corrosion, or, as it is most generally known, oxidation. When a metal such as aluminum is exposed to a gas containing oxygen, a chemical reaction takes place at the surface between the metal and the gas. In this case, two aluminum atoms join three oxygen atoms to form aluminum oxide:

$$2\,Al + 3\,O \rightarrow Al_2O_3$$

If the metal is iron or steel (ferrous metal), two atoms of iron will join three atoms of oxygen and form iron oxide or rust:

$$2\,Fe + 3\,O \rightarrow Fe_2O_3$$

There is one big difference between iron oxide and aluminum oxide. The film of aluminum oxide is unbroken, and once it is formed, further reaction with the oxygen continues at a greatly reduced rate; almost stops. Iron oxide, on the other hand, forms a porous or interrupted film, and the metal will continue to react with the oxygen in the air until the metal is completely eaten away.

In order to protect iron from dry corrosion or rusting, the best procedure is to prevent oxygen coming into contact with the surface. This may be done temporarily by covering the surface with oil or grease, or for more permanent protection, with a coat of paint.

Aluminum alloy may be protected from oxidation by the formation of an oxide film on its surface. This film insulates the aluminum from any electrolyte (gas or liquid), and will not, itself, further react with the oxygen. The formation of this film is discussed in detail in methods of corrosion treatment under the headings of anodizing and Alodining.

## B. Uniform Surface Corrosion

Where an area of unprotected metal is exposed to an atmosphere containing battery fumes, exhaust gases, or industrial contaminants, there will be a rather uniform attack over the entire surface area. This dulling of the surface is caused by microscopic amounts of the metal being converted into corrosion salts. If these deposits are not removed and the surface protected against further action, there will develop such a rough surface that corrosion pits will form.

## C. Pitting

A logical progression from uniform surface corrosion, if left untreated, is called pitting. Pits form as localized anodic areas. Corrosive action may continue until an appreciable percentage of the metal thickness is converted into salts which may, in extreme cases, eat completely through the metal. Pitting corrosion may be detected by the appearance of clumps of white powder on the surface.

## D. Intergranular Corrosion

Micro-photographs of aluminum alloys show them made up of extremely tiny grains held together by chemical bonds; that is, the interaction of the atoms of the various elements. In the process of heat treating, the metal is heated to such a temperature that these alloying agents go into solution with each other. When this temperature has been reached uniformly throughout, the metal is removed from the furnace and immediately quenched in water to solidify these elements into extremely small grains. If quenching is delayed, for even a few seconds, these grains will grow, and when finally quenched, will have reached such size that the areas of dissimilar metals will provide efficient cathodes and anodes for corrosion formation.

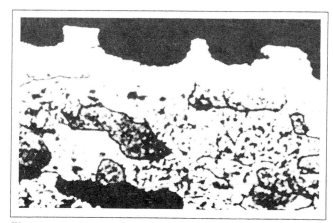

*Figure 2-1. Pitting corrosion.*

5

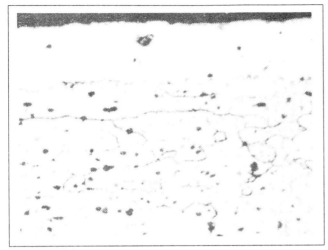

*Figure 2-2. Metal grain structure.*

If then through a pit, corrosive action reaches the boundary between the enlarged grains, the action can continue within the metal. The electrolyte for this action is supplied from the surface through the corrosion deposits, and along the grain boundaries as intergranular corrosion continues. Spot welds or seam welds can also cause grain enlargement to the extent that it leaves the metal susceptible to intergranular corrosion. Beneath the surface, removed from the point of initial penetration, there may occur small blisters. The surface metal over these blisters is quite thin, and when picked with a knife point, show a cavity filled with the salts of corrosion. Intergranular corrosion, since it is within the metal itself, rather than on the surface, is difficult to detect without ultrasonic or X-ray equipment. Just about the only practical and sure fix for intergranular corrosion is replacement of the part.

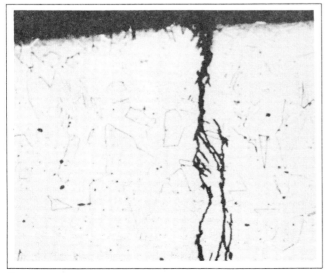

*Figure 2-3. Intergranular corrosion.*

## E. Exfoliation Corrosion

This type of corrosion, despite its high sounding name, is simply an extreme case of intergranular corrosion. It occurs chiefly in extruded materials such as channels or angles where the grain structure is more laminar (layer-like) than in rolled sheets or castings. This type of corrosion occurs along the grain boundaries and causes the material to separate or delaminate. As with other types of intergranular corrosion, by the time it is evident on the surface, the strength of the metal has been greatly decreased.

## F. Galvanic Corrosion

This common type of corrosion occurs any time these two conditions are present:

1. Two dissimilar metals are connected in such a way as to provide a path for electron flow.
2. Their common surfaces are covered with some material to serve as an electrolyte.

This action can take place where dissimilar metal skins are riveted together, or where aluminum inspection plates are attached to the structure with steel screws.

When metals of the same galvanic grouping, Figure 2-6, are joined together, they show little tendency for galvanic corrosion. But, metals of one group will certainly corrode when held in contact with another group. The further apart the groups, the more active the corrosion. The materials of the lower numbered group will be the anode of the galvanic pair, and will be the one corroded. In the example of a steel screw being used to hold an aluminum alloy inspection plate in place: if contaminated moisture gets between the two metals the aluminum will form corrosion products and be eaten away. If, on the other hand, 2024-T3 aluminum alloy and magnesium are held together in the presence of an

*Figure 2-4. Exfoliation corrosion.*

electrolyte, the magnesium will be corroded because it is in a lower numbered group than aluminum alloy.

# G. Concentration Cell Corrosion

## 1. Oxygen concentration cell

When water ($H_2O$) covers the surface of a metal such as aluminum airplane skins, and some seeps into the cracks between the lap joints of the sheets, concentration cell corrosion may form: since water in an open area readily absorbs oxygen from the air, it then attracts electrons from the metal to form negative hydroxide ions:

$$2\ H_2O\ \&\ O_2\ \&\ 4\ electrons \rightarrow 4(OH)$$

Two molecules of water plus one molecule of oxygen plus four electrons will form four negative hydroxide ions. This is according to a basic law of chemistry.

The electrons required to form these negative ions come from the metal itself. The area between the skins does not give up electrons to the water on its surface because there is not enough oxygen there to form hydroxide ions. Its electrons flow instead to the cathodic surface — the open area. The area between the skins, having lost electrons, now has positive aluminum ions, and has become the anode.

As we have seen, electrons flow within the metal from the anode to the cathode, leaving positive metal ions in the area between the sheets. This positive aluminum attracts the negative hydroxide ions from the open water and corrodes, forming aluminum hydroxide. The unusual characteristic of this type of corrosion is that it forms in the areas where there is a deficiency of oxygen.

Oxygen cell corrosion can occur on aluminum, magnesium, or ferrous metals. It forms under marking tape or ferrules on aluminum tubing, beneath sealer that has loosened, or under bolt or screw heads.

When dirt or other oxygen-excluding contaminants form on an anodized surface, and the oxide film is scratched, oxygen concentration cell corrosion can prevent the reformation of the protective film.

## 2. Metallic ion concentration cell

The electrode potential within a metal is dependent on the different metals that make up the alloy, but a potential difference can be caused if an electrolyte having a differing concentration of metal ions covers the surface. In Figure 2-8, the surface of an aircraft is covered with a film of water. As was true in oxygen cell corrosion, when water absorbs oxygen, it takes electrons from the metal and forms negative hydroxide ions. When these electrons were taken from the aluminum, it left positive aluminum ions. The open area on the surface of the metal is free for the water to move, and continually carry the aluminum ions away, while the water between the skins in the faying surfaces cannot have its ion concentration diluted. The water (electrolyte) between the skins therefore has a higher concentration of metal ions than that on the open skin. The skin area of the faying surface where the concentration of positive metal ions is the highest becomes the cathode and attracts electrons from the skin in the open area, the anode. As electrons flow from the anode to the cathode, they leave positive aluminum ions on the surface near the supply of negative hydroxide ions. These hydroxide ions join the aluminum ions to form aluminum hydroxide corrosion.

Notice the difference between the two types of concentration cell corrosion: the metal ion concentration cell corrosion forms in the closed area between the faying surfaces. Corrosion on airplanes is usually complex, and is composed of more than one type.

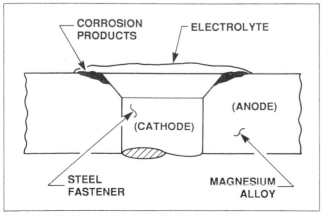

*Figure 2-5. Galvanic corrosion.*

| GROUP I | MAGNESIUM AND ITS ALLOYS; ALUMINUM ALLOYS 5052, 5056, 5356, 6061, AND 6063. |
|---|---|
| GROUP II | CADMIUM, ZINC, AND ALUMINUM AND THEIR ALLOYS EXCEPT THE ALUMINUM ALLOYS IN GROUP I. |
| GROUP III | IRON, LEAD, AND TIN AND THEIR ALLOYS EXCEPT STAINLESS STEEL. |
| GROUP IV | COPPER, CHROMIUM, NICKEL, SILVER, GOLD, PLATINUM, TITANIUM, COBALT, AND RHODIUM AND THEIR ALLOYS, STAINLESS STEEL AND GRAPHITE. |

*Figure 2-6. Galvanic grouping of metals.*

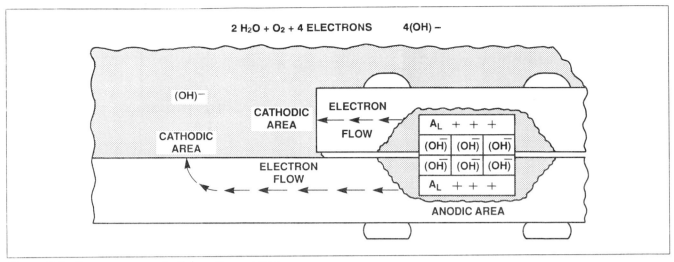

$$2 H_2O + O_2 + 4 \text{ ELECTRONS} \quad 4(OH) -$$

Figure 2-7. Oxygen concentration cell corrosion.

## H. Stress Corrosion

Another special type of intergranular corrosion is stress corrosion. This occurs when the metal is subjected to a tensile stress in the presence of a corrosive environment. The stresses in the metal may come from improper quenching after heat treatment, or from interference (press) fit of a fastener. Cracks caused by stress corrosion grow rapidly as the corrosive attack concentrates at the end of the crack rather than along its sides.

Since stress corrosion can occur only in the presence of tensile stresses, one expedient for preventing this type of corrosion in some heat treated aluminum alloy parts is to shot peen the surface to provide a uniformly compressive stressed surface. These stresses must be overcome by tensile forces before stress corrosion can occur.

A common place for stress corrosion is between rivets in a stressed skin, around pressed-in bushing, or tapered pipe fittings. Careful visual inspection may show up this type of corrosion, but to find the actual extent of the cracks requires dye penetrant inspection.

## I. Fretting Corrosion

When two surfaces fit tightly together, but can move relative to one another, they may be eroded. These

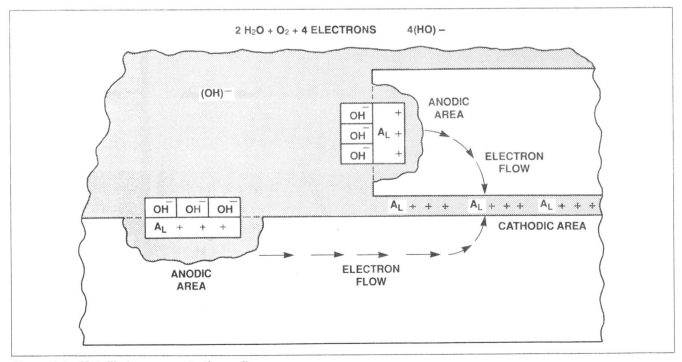

$$2 H_2O + O_2 + 4 \text{ ELECTRONS} \quad 4(HO) -$$

Figure 2-8. Metallic ion concentration cell.

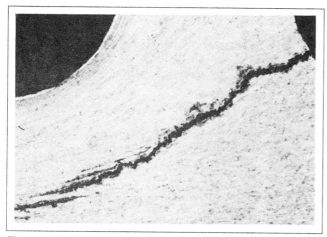

Figure 2-9. Stress corrosion crack.

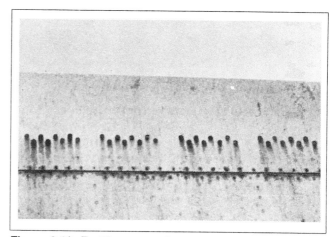

Figure 2-10. Fretting corrosion.

surfaces are normally not close enough together to shut out oxygen so they do develop the desired protective film. However, this film is destroyed by the continued rubbing action. This wear is fretting corrosion. When movement between the two surfaces is small, the debris between them does not have an opportunity to escape, and it acts as an abrasive to further erode the surfaces. By the time this type of corrosion makes its appearance on the surface, the

damage is usually done and the parts must be replaced. Application of the proper lubricant can minimize this type of damage.

Fretting corrosion may occur around rivets in a skin. This will be indicated by dark deposits around the rivet heads, streaming out behind. It gives the appearance of the rivet smoking. Rivets showing this sign of fretting must be replaced as soon as possible.

# Study Questions:

1. What is meant by dry corrosion?

2. What is the basic difference between the growth of aluminum oxide and iron oxide, or rust?

3. How is a steel part generally protected from rust?

4. What will usually develop if uniform surface corrosion of an aluminum alloy is not checked?

5. How does a corrosion pit show up?

6. How does improper quenching of a heat treated aluminum alloy part cause the piece to be susceptible to intergranular corrosion?

7. How does intergranular corrosion usually show up in an aluminum alloy structure?

8. What type of inspection in usually required to detect intergranular corrosion?

9. What form of repair is normally required of a piece of metal in which intergranular corrosion is found?

10. In what form of aluminum alloy does exfoliation corrosion usually develop?

11. If an unplated copper bonding braid is attached to an aluminum alloy structure and not protected, which will corrode, the aluminum or the copper?

12. Does oxygen concentration cell corrosion form at a point of high or low oxygen concentration?

13. What type of stress is necessary for the formation of stress corrosion?

14. Can fretting corrosion occur if the joint is completely air tight?

15. What should be done to rivets showing signs of fretting corrosion?

# Chapter III

# Causes of Corrosion

## A. Acids and Alkalis

For corrosion to form on a metal, there must be an electrode potential difference and an electrolyte. Almost all acids and alkalis react with metals to form metallic salts (corrosion), though some are more active than others. Sulfuric acid as found in batteries is especially active in corroding aluminum, while a weak solution of chromic or phosphoric acid is actually used as a surface treatment when preparing a metal for painting.

Ferrous metals are subject to damage from both acids and alkalis, but aluminum is more vulnerable to strong alkaline solutions than to acids. Aluminum structure, for instance, can be severely corroded if allowed to remain on a concrete floor. Water will leach out enough lime from the cement to form an alkaline solution that will corrode the aluminum.

## B. Salts

Marine atmosphere and air above some of the industrial areas hold a large concentration of salts. These chemicals will precipitate out of the air and form on the surface of an airplane. They then attract water and form an effective electrolyte on the metal. Magnesium is especially subject to corrosive attack from an electrolyte formed by salt solutions.

## C. Mercury

Although it is not commonly found in any quantity around aircraft, there is a definite possibility that mercury could be spilled in an airplane. Mercury attacks aluminum by a chemical reaction known as amalgamation. In this process, the mercury rapidly attacks along the grain boundaries of the aluminum, and in an exceedingly short time will completely destroy it. Extreme care must be exercised when removing spilled mercury, as it is "slippery" and will flow through even a tiny crack to get to the lowest part of the structure where it can cause extensive damage. Not only is mercury damaging to aircraft structure, mercury and mercury vapors are also dangerous to people. If mercury is spilled, remove every particle with a vacuum cleaner having a mercury trap in the suction line, or with a rubber suction bulb or medicine dropper. Never attempt to remove mercury by blowing with compressed air. This will scatter it and spread the damage.

Brass control cable turnbuckle barrels are especially susceptible to mercury damage. Any sign of mercury discoloration requires replacement of the barrel.

## D. Water

Pure water will react with metals to cause corrosion or oxidation, but water holding a concentration of salts or other contaminants will cause much more rapid corrosion. Seaplanes are continually in a battle with the elements, and every precaution must be taken to stay ahead of the formation of corrosion. Seaplanes operating in salt water are especially vulnerable to attack. When a seaplane is taken out of the water it should be hosed down with large volumes of fresh water to get every trace of salt off of the structure. Seaplane ramps are often in areas where the water has a concentration of industrial wastes which make the water more corrosive. The bottom of floats and flying boat hulls are subject to the abrasive effect of high velocity water on takeoffs and landings. This tends to damage the natural protective oxide film. Seaplanes must be carefully inspected to detect any damage which would allow water to get to the base metal of the structure.

## E. Air

Naturally it is impossible to isolate the structure of an aircraft from the air in which it exists, but the very presence of the air is a factor in the deterioration of the metal. Airborne salts and other chemical compounds settle onto the surface of an airplane and attract moisture from the air. Corrosion then has its key prerequisite, an electrolyte.

## F. Organic Growths

New developments bring new problems. For years, water which condensed in the fuel tanks produced relatively minor corrosion problems. Small perforated metal containers of potassium dichromate crystals protected the fuel tanks by changing any water into a mild chromic acid solution which inhibited corrosion. Jet aircraft, however, use fuel with a higher viscosity than gasoline, fuel which holds more water in suspension. They also fly higher than reciprocating engine aircraft. In high altitude, low temperature flight conditions, the water entrained in the fuel will condense out and collect in the bottom of the tanks. To further complicate matters, this water contains microbes which are simply microscopic sized animal life and plant life. These organic bodies live in the water and feed on the hydrocarbon fuel. The dark insides of the fuel tanks promote their growth, and before you know it, these tiny creatures have multiplied until they form a scum in the tank. It holds water in contact with the tank structure where corrosion of the concentration cell type will inevitably form. If the scum forms along the edge of a seal in an integral fuel tank, the sealant may pull away from the structure, causing a leak and an expensive resealing operation.

It is virtually impossible to prevent this type of growth if bacteria and other microbes are allowed to live in the fuel, so the successful approach to this problem has been to use an additive in the fuel which kills these "bugs" and prevents the formation of the

**Figure 3-1. Extensive corrosion damage from exposure to agricultural chemicals.**

corrosion-forming scum. In addition to preventing corrosion by its biocidal action, this same fuel additive has the additional useful function of serving as an anti-freeze agent for water which has been freed from the fuel.

# Study Questions

1. Who is aluminum likely to corrode if left on a concrete floor?

2. Why should mercury not be allowed to come into contact with aluminum?

3. What can be done to a seaplane to prevent corrosion from the salt water?

4. What forms the scum on the bottom of some jet aircraft fuel tanks?

5. How can the scum in jet aircraft fuel tanks cause corrosion?

6. How can an additive in the fuel help prevent corrosion in a fuel tank?

# Chapter IV

# Locations for Corrosion

Modern airplanes are made of thin, reactive metals which can tolerate very little loss of strength. One of the most important functions of the A&P technician on an annual or 100 hour inspection is to check the entire structure for indications of corrosion which could degrade the strength of the airplane. Almost all parts of an airplane are subject to this type of damage, but certain areas are more prone than others.

## A. Engine Exhaust Area

Both reciprocating and turbine engines generate their power by converting chemical energy from a hydrocarbon fuel into heat energy. Because of the inefficiency of the engine, much of these heat and energy-rich gases pass out of the engine through the exhaust. These gases contain all of the constituents for a potent electrolyte, and because of their elevated temperature, corrosion can form all the more rapidly. Exhaust areas must be carefully inspected and all exhaust residue removed before corrosion has a chance to start. Cracks and seams in the exhaust track are prime areas for corrosion. Fairings of the nacelles, hinges and fasteners on inspection doors all contain crevices which invite the formation of corrosion.

## B. Battery Compartments and Vents

Almost all airplanes nowadays have an electrical system and a battery. These batteries store electrical energy by converting it into chemical energy, and are therefore active chemical plants complete with environment-polluting exhausts. Airplanes having lead-acid batteries must have their boxes protected by a material that resists corrosion from the sulfuric acid fumes, and airplanes with nickel-cadmium batteries must have their battery areas protected with an alkaline resistant finish. These finishes usually have a bitumastic (tar) base or a rubber base.

On an inspection, these areas must be carefully checked, especially under the battery, and any trace of corrosion removed and the areas refinished. Both types of batteries should have a vent sump jar containing a pad moist with a neutralizing agent, bicarbonate of soda for the lead-acid battery, and boric acid for the nickel-cadmium battery. These sump jars should be checked to see that the pads are moist, and that there is no leakage. All of the vent openings should be clear and the intake and exhaust lines free and open. If battery electrolyte is spilled during servicing it must be cleaned up immediately, and the area neutralized. Flush with water and neutralize with bicarbonate of soda for lead-acid, or boric acid Or vinegar for nickel-cadmium installation. The thoroughness of the neutralization can be checked with a piece of litmus paper. Blot the water on the surface with a piece of this indicator paper. If the area is acidic, the paper will turn pink; if it is alkaline, it will turn blue. The entire area should be neutral and not change the color of the paper.

## C. Lavatories and Food Service Areas

Organic materials such as food and human wastes are highly corrosive to aluminum surfaces, and the areas where this type of material may be spilled must be inspected with extreme care. Food service areas may be troublesome if there is a possibility of some of the debris from food getting into cracks under or behind the galley where it cannot be removed. ale this material, in itself, may not be corrosive, it can hold water which will cause the structure to corrode. The lavatory area is an especially important area to check for corrosion. Human wastes are usually acidic and promote corrosion in a hurry if allowed to remain on the skin of the airplane or to get into cracks or seams in the structure. Disinfectants may be used that will cause further damage to the aircraft. Be sure to check the disinfectant carried in the airplane, that it is not of a type harmful to aluminum.

Airplanes having relief tubes must have the area around and behind the discharge inspected carefully for indication of corrosion. These areas may be painted with an acid proof paint where the discharge contacts the airplane skin.

## D. Wheel Wells and Landing Gear

Probably no one area of an airplane is subjected to as much hard service as the wheel well area. On takeoff and landing, debris from the runway surface may be thrown up into this area. This can be especially troublesome in the winter, where chemicals are used on runways for ice control. Abrasives may remove the protective lubricants and coatings. Water and mud can freeze and cause damage from the ice formation. Corrosion can take place in any of the electrical components such as anti-skid sensors, squat switches, and limit switches. Bolt heads and nuts on magnesium wheels are susceptible to galvanic corrosion. Concentration cell corrosion can form under the marking tape on aluminum tubing. Special care must be taken to search out any area where water can be entrapped.

## E. External Skin Areas

### 1. Seams and lap joints

One of the first places corrosion appears on the surfaces of an aircraft is along the seams and lap joints. It is here that concentration cell corrosion frequently appears, and in clad skins, it is here that the sheared edges expose the alloy without the protection of the pure aluminum. There is a danger of water or cleaning solvents becoming entrapped in the lap joints and providing an effective electrolyte.

Spot welded seams may have the start of corrosion caused by the spot welding process leaving an enlarged grain structure in the metal. The area is susceptible to further corrosion when moisture seeps between the skins. Check carefully for bulging along the spot welds. Hold a straightedge along the row of spots. If there is corrosion in the seams, the skin will bulge between the spots, and show up as a wavy skin. Corrosion in a seam can progress to such a degree that the spots actually pull apart.

## 2. Engine inlet areas

One of the most vital parts of an airplane is the area directly in front of the engine where air is taken in. In jet aircraft, this area is usually quite large, and air rushes into the engine at a high velocity. Abrasion by this high velocity air and contaminants carried in the air will tend to remove any protective coating. Abrasion strips along the leading edges of intake ducts help protect these areas, but careful inspection and maintenance of the finish in these inlet areas is imperative.

## F. Inaccessible Areas

### 1. Fuel tanks

There is probably no single place on an airplane less accessible for inspection and repair than an integral fuel tank; yet, especially on jet aircraft, the fuel tanks are places where corrosion is highly likely to form. As discussed in the area on organic growths as a cause of corrosion, we saw that turbine fuel can hold microscopic "bugs" in suspension until they have an opportunity to join together and grow into the water-holding scum which attaches to the aluminum alloy skin. Sealants used to make the structure of a wing into a fuel tank are impervious to fuel, but only resistant to water. It is possible for water to seep through the sealer and cause oxygen concentration cell corrosion. Corrosion in this location is extremely difficult to detect and must usually be found with X-ray or ultrasonic inspection from the outside of the wing.

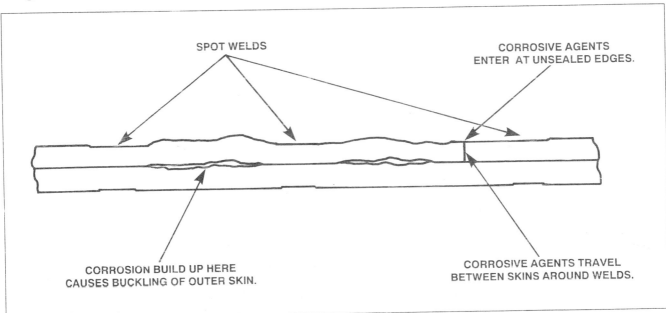

*Figure 4-1. Spot welded seams are a likely place for corrosion to form.*

## 2. Piano hinges

Piano hinges on control surfaces and access doors offer ideal conditions for the start and development of corrosion. The hinge body is usually made of aluminum alloy and the pin of hard carbon steel. Coupled with the fact that these are dissimilar metals, it is almost impossible to keep the cracks and crevices free from moisture.

Dirt and dust accumulate and hold moisture between the pin and the hinge body, allowing corrosion to develop. The pin may rust and freeze in the hinge, even breaking off and becoming impossible to remove. Piano hinges should be kept as clean and dry as possible, and lubricated with a spray which displaces water and leaves an extremely thin film of lubricant; one that will not gum or attract dust. These water-displacing lubricants are manufactured to meet MIL- C-16173 specification.

## 3. Control surface recesses

Any place on an airplane which is difficult to inspect is an area where corrosion has an opportunity to grow. Some airplanes have areas in the wing or empennage where the movable surfaces recess back into the fixed surface.

Hinges are buried back in these cavities and are difficult to lubricate. Special attention must be paid when inspecting these areas to remove every trace of corrosion, and provide drains for any water that might collect. A thin film of the same water displacing lubricant used on piano hinges may be used to protect the skin lap joints in these recesses.

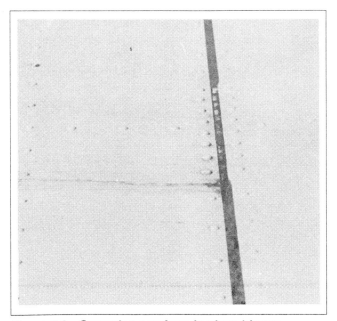

*Figure 4-2. Corrosion can form in piano hinges.*

## 4. Bilges

The bottom of the fuselage, below the floor boards, is an area where water and all forms of liquid and solid debris can accumulate and cause corrosion to form. These areas are not only ideal for the formation of corrosion because they provide the dissimilar metals and constant exposure to an electrolyte, but because of their inaccessibility, corrosion can often go undetected until it has caused major damage. Airplanes having areas prone to accumulate water have drain holes provided, but since dirt and other debris also collect here, these holes may become clogged and not do their job. On every inspection, be sure all drain holes are clear, and inspect carefully any area where water might possibly stand. Air powered vacuum cleaners may be used to remove dirt or water collected in these areas. A water displacing liquid spray will form a thin film on the surface of the metal and prevent further contact with the electrolyte.

## 5. Landing gear boxes

There are few areas in a modern fixed gear airplane that are as highly stressed, yet as difficult to inspect as the landing gear box structure. The landing gear attaches into the fuselage by a strong, heavy gage aluminum alloy box. This structure is under the floor where it is accessible for inspection only through a relatively small access hole. Water can collect in this area if the drain holes become plugged. Inspection of these boxes should be thorough, all drains opened, and the entire enclosed area generously sprayed with a water displacing lubricant film.

## G. Engine Mount Structure

The heavy current from the starter must return to the battery through the engine mount. This current

*Figure 4-3. Control surface recesses are likely places for corrosion to form.*

flowing through joints in an aluminum alloy mount will create the potential difference required for corrosion and cause it to form in these areas.

Welded steel tube mounts are protected from corrosion by filling each tube with hot linseed oil or other type of tubing oil. Allow as much oil to drain out as will, then plug the hole with a drive screw or self tapping metal screw.

## H. Control Cables

The cables used in aircraft control systems may be made of either carbon steel or corrosion resistant steel. If carbon steel cables are left unprotected and water allowed to enter, it will soon corrode, and the corrosion that forms inside the cable will be difficult to detect. If corrosion is suspected, the cable should

Figure 4-4. *Landing gear boxes should be carefully inspected for traces of corrosion.*

have its tension released, and the strands opened up by twisting against the lay. This allows you to see between the strands. Cable with any indications of corrosion should be replaced.

Corrosion may be prevented by spraying the cable with a water displacing type of lubricant, or if it is used in a seaplane, or exposed to agricultural chemicals, it should be coated with a waxy grease such as Par-al-ketone.

## I. Welded Areas

Aluminum welding requires the use of a flux to exclude oxygen from the weld. This flux may contain lithium chloride, potassium chloride, potassium bisulphide or potassium fluoride. These are extremely corrosive to aluminum, and all traces of the flux must be removed after welding is completed. Welding flux is soluble in water and may be removed with hot water and a nonmetallic bristle brush.

## J. Electronic Equipment

The use of copper, lead, tin, and other metals in electronic wiring and printed circuit boards makes them a target for corrosion. The fact that electrons are continually flowing in these conductors and the extremely low tolerance for corrosion make corrosion control in these areas vital. This is usually done by coating the wiring and circuit boards with a transparent film which excludes all oxygen and moisture from the surface. Detection and repair of corrosion in these areas is a highly specialized field and will not be attempted by most A&P technicians.

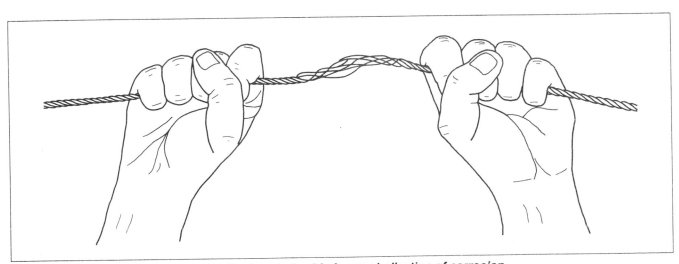

Figure 4-5. *Inspect between the strands of control cable for any indication of corrosion.*

# Study Questions

1. Why are skins in the engine exhaust areas particularly subject to corrosion?

2. Name three places in an exhaust area that should be carefully inspected for corrosion formation.

3. What type of finish is used to protect the inside of a battery box against corrosion?

4. What is used to neutralize lead-acid battery fumes?

5. What is used to neutralize nickel-cadmium battery fumes?

6. What is the purpose of the sump-jar in a battery compartment vent system?

7. How can noncorrosive food spilled behind a galley cause corrosion of the structure?

8. What is indicated if blue litmus paper turns pink when it is placed in water which has been used to rinse a battery compartment?

9. Name two reasons wheel well areas are especially vulnerable to corrosion attack.

10. Name three places corrosion is likely to form in the landing gear area of an airplane.

11. Who are spot welded seams especially susceptible to corrosion formation?

12. How can corrosion be detected in a spot welded seam?

13. How can corrosion in a piano hinge be minimized?

14. What can be used to protect hard-to-get-to areas in a control surface recess from corrosion in the hinges and skin lap joints?

15. Why is it important that all drain holes in bilge areas be open?

16. How may the inside of a landing gear box structure be protected against corrosion?

17. Who are engine mount structures especially prone to corrosion attack?

18. What is done to protect the inside of a welded steel tube engine mount from corrosion?

19. How may control cables be inspected for internal corrosion?

20. What type of corrosion preventative is used on control cables?

21. How may welding flux be removed from aluminum?

22. How are electronic printed circuit boards protected from corrosion?

# Chapter V

# Detecting Corrosion

## A. Visual Inspection

Exotic inspection equipment is often used for certain parts of an aircraft to make the work of the A&P more efficient, but the old fashioned eyeball is still the most effective tool for inspection. Corrosion can often be detected by a careful visual inspection of the airplane structure. Corrosion of aluminum or magnesium appears as a white or gray powder along the edge of skins, or around rivet heads. Small blisters appearing under the finish on painted surfaces indicate corrosion. Examine lap joints in the skins for bulges which indicate corrosion forming between the faying surfaces. Corrosion salts have more volume than aluminum and will push out against the skin. The complex structure of modern aircraft makes the use of magnifying glasses, mirrors, borescopes, fiber optics, and other tools for seeing around corners imperative for a good visual inspection.

## B. Dye Penetrant Inspection

Stress corrosion cracks are sometimes difficult, if not impossible, to detect by visual inspection. These cracks may be found by the use of dye penetrant inspection, however. This inspection method is effective on ferrous or non- ferrous metals and non-porous plastics. The principle of this type inspection is that of spraying a penetrating liquid on the surface to be inspected. This material has a very low surface tension and will seep deep into any crack that extends to the surface. After this liquid has had sufficient time to penetrate, the surface is wiped clean of all liquid, and a developer sprayed on. This developer is a white chalky powder that completely covers the surface and acts as a blotter to draw penetrant out of any cracks in the material. The penetrant is usually dyed bright red, and cracks appear as red lines on the white surface. Another type of penetrant inspection uses a fluorescent penetrant and is viewed under an ultraviolet or "black light". Cracks appear as green lines on the surface under this special light. The limitation of dye penetrant inspection is the fact that it can fail to show cracks that are so full of corrosion products that the dye cannot penetrate. Also, if the crack is filled with oil or grease, the penetrant cannot get in, and there will be no indication of a flaw. Porous or rough surfaces are almost impossible to clean of all the penetrant, and do not lend themselves to this type of inspection.

## C. Ultrasonic Inspection

One inspection method that has recently been applied to corrosion inspection is that using ultrasonic energy. In this method of inspection, high frequency pulses of energy, similar to sound waves, only at frequencies far above the audible range, actually from about 0.5 megahertz to 25 megahertz (500,000 cycles to 25,000,000 cycles per second) are introduced into the airplane structure. There are two types of readouts which may be used for corrosion detection; the pulse-echo method and the resonance method. In the pulse-echo method, a pulse of ultrasonic energy is introduced into the structure; this energy travels through the material to the opposite side, then bounces back. When return pulse is received by the transducer, it is displayed on the screen of a cathode ray oscilloscope, as a spike which establishes the time base, representing the thickness of the material. If there is any change in thickness, as may be caused by corrosion, the return will occupy a shorter space and will thus indicate the amount of damage. If there should be a crack or other flaw within the material, such as may be caused by intergranular corrosion, a second spike will appear on the oscilloscope screen and indicate the approximate position of the flaw within the material.

The second method of inspection using ultrasonics is the resonance method. This operates on the basis that for a given thickness material, there will be a specific frequency of ultrasonic energy that

*Figure 5-1. Dye penetrant inspection can detect cracks that extend to the surface.*

*Figure 5-2. Ultrasonic method of crack or fault detection.*

will resonate or produce the greatest amount of return. Variable frequency ultrasonic energy is fed into the transducer and the output is monitored either with a meter, or audibly with a set of headphones. When the resonant frequency is reached, the meter will read the highest value, or the tone will be the loudest in the phones. If the metal has been eaten away by corrosion, the resonant frequency will be different and the meter reading or tone volume will be lower. The resonance method can be used to determine the actual thickness of the material by calibrating the probe with a test specimen of the same type material being tested. Ultrasonic inspections must be conducted by a person highly qualified and equipped for this procedure. False returns can easily disguise a fault, and many special transducers are needed for the different locations to be inspected. Ultrasonic inspection is primarily inspection by comparison. Good skin is measured and any change in thickness may be caused by corrosion. Further inspection must be made to determine the actual extent of the corrosion indicated by ultrasonics.

## D. X-Ray

Like ultrasonic inspection, X-ray is used to deter mine from the outside of a structure if there is damage on the inside. X-ray is a photographic form of inspection in which extremely high frequency pulses of electromagnetic radiation are passed through the structure being inspected. Energy at this frequency has the ability to expose photographic film. As it passes through the structure, areas of high density pass less of the radiation energy and expose the film less. After the exposure, the film is developed as any other photographic negative. In areas where the density of the material is greatest, less energy will penetrate and it will appear light on the negative. Areas where density is less pass more energy, ex pose the film more, and appear darker. X-ray inspection requires extensive training and experience or proper interpretation of the results. The use of X-ray involves some danger because exposure to radiation energy used in this process may cause burns, damage to the blood, and possible death. Persons around X-ray equipment should wear a radiation monitor film badge which is developed at the end of an exposure time to determine the amount of radiation the wearer has absorbed. A blood count should be made periodically for persons involved in X-ray inspections. The amount of penetration by X-ray is determined by the amount of power used. This is normally expressed in terms of kilovolts applied to the X-ray tube, and may range from about 8 kilovolts to as much as 200 kilovolts. The lower powered applications, called "soft" X-rays, are used in inspections for corrosion.

# Study Questions

1. What is the most important tool to use in corrosion detection?

2. What are the three steps used in the dye penetrant method of inspection?

3. What is a limitation to the use of dye penetrants for corrosion detection?

4. Can dye penetrant be used on a steel part to detect a surface crack?

5. Name two methods of detecting corrosion damage by ultrasonic inspection.

6. What are two limitations to the use of ultrasonic inspection for corrosion damage?

7. In an X-ray inspection, will an area of corrosion damage appear light or dark on the photographic negative?

8. How can an X-ray operator determine that he has not been exposed to an excessive amount of radiation?

9. What determines the amount an X-ray inspection will penetrate the structure?

10. Are X-rays of high power or low power used in inspection for corrosion?

# Chapter VI

# Removing and Treating Corrosion

## A. Surface Preparation

### 1. Cleaning

The first and most important step on corrosion control is a thorough cleaning of the airplane. An emulsion.type cleaner that meets MIL-C-25769 specification does an excellent job of removing grime, dirt, exhaust residue, and dried oil and grease deposits. The airplane should be parked on a wash rack or an area where it can be hosed down, and preferably in an area where the sun will not dry the surface before the cleaner has had time to penetrate the film. For the main part of the exterior of the airplane, use a 1:5 or a 1:3 dilution of the cleaner with water. Brush or spray the cleaner on the surface and allow it to stand for a few minutes, then rinse with a high pressure stream of water, preferably warm.

Engine cowling and wheel well areas usually have grease or oil deposits that this treatment will not remove, so they must be soaked with a 1:2 dilution of the emulsion cleaner. After allowing the cleaner to soak for a few minutes, scrub with a soft bristle brush to completely loosen the film, and rinse with a high pressure stream of warm water.

Stubborn exhaust stains require a 1:2 mixture of the cleaner with varsol or kerosine. Mix these to a creamy emulsion and apply to the surface. Let it stand for a few minutes and work all of the loosened residue with a bristle brush and hose it off with a high pressure stream of warm water. This treatment can be repeated if the first time does not get all of the stains.

### 2. Paint removal

After completely cleaning the structure, if corrosion does exist, the damage must be assessed, and a decision made to determine what action to take. All corrosion products must be removed as soon as they are discovered because corrosion will continue as long as they remain on the surface.

Corrosion on a painted surface cannot be inspected thoroughly without first removing all of the paint. Before using any paint remover with which you are not familiar, first test it on a piece of metal similar to that with which you will be working. If it does not have adverse effects, it is safe to used. All areas not to be stripped should be masked to prevent stripper accidently coming into contact with these

areas. Water rinsable paint removers of a syrupy consistency are usually best for aircraft surfaces. This type of remover is applied with a brush by daubing it on the surface, not brushing it on. Cover the surface with a heavy coating of remover, and allow it to stand until the paint swells and wrinkles up. This breaks the bond between the surface and the finish. It may be necessary to reapply the remover; if so, scrape the old paint away with a plastic or aluminum scraper, and apply the second treatment. This allows the active chemicals to get to the lower layers of the finish. After all of the finish has swelled up and broken away from the surface, it should be rinsed off with hot water or live steam. A stiff bristle brush will most probably have to be used around rivet heads and along the seams to get all the stubborn paint that adheres to these places.

Caution must be observed whenever you use any paint remover. Many solvents used in paint removers attack rubber and synthetic rubber pro ducts. Tires, hoses, and seals must be protected from contact with paint removers. These solvents are also highly toxic, and special care must be observed that none of them get into the skin or in the eyes. If paint remover is spilled or splashed on the skin, the area must be flushed with water immediately. If any gets into your eyes, flood the eyes with water and get to a doctor as soon as possible.

## B. Treatment of Aluminum Alloy

### 1. Mechanical corrosion removal

After all of the paint has been removed, all traces of corrosion products, the white powder, must be removed from the surface.

Very mild corrosion may be removed by using a household abrasive cleaner such as Bon-Ami. Be sure that the abrasive does not contain chlorine. Nylon scrubbers such as Scotch-Brite can be used to remove this mild corrosion.

More severe, but not heavy corrosion can be removed by brushing with aluminum wool or an aluminum wire brush.

Caution: Do not use a steel wire brush or steel wool, as traces of the steel will imbed in the aluminum and cause severe corrosion. Blasting the surface with glass beads smaller that 500 mesh can be used to remove corrosion from the pits. After using abrasives or brushing, examine the metal with a five- to ten-power magnifying glass to make sure that all traces of corrosion have been removed.

Severely corroded aluminum alloys must be given more drastic treatment to remove all of the corrosion. Rotary files or power grinders using rubber wheels impregnated with aluminum oxide may be used to grind out every trace of corrosion damage. Watch carefully to see that the minimum amount of material is removed but that all of the damage has been cleaned out. After an examination with a five- to ten-power magnifying glass shows no trace of corrosion remaining, remove about two thousandths inch more material to be sure that the ends of intergranular cracks have been reached, and then sand the area smooth with 280 grit, then 400 grit abrasive paper. Clean the area with solvent or an emulsion cleaner, and treat the surface with an inhibitor such as Alodine®.

## 2. Chemical neutralization

After removing all of the corrosion products possible, the surface should be treated with a 5% chromic acid solution to neutralize any remaining corrosion salts. After the acid has been on the surface for at least five minutes, it should be washed off with water and allowed to dry. Alodine treatment conforming to MIL-C-5541 will neutralize the corrosion as well as forming a protective film on the surface of the metal. Its application is discussed under the heading of Surface Oxide Film-Chemical Treatment.

## 3. Protective coating

### a. Cladding

Pure aluminum is considered to be noncorrosive. This is not altogether true, because aluminum readily acts with the oxygen in the air to form an oxide film.

This film is so dense that it does not allow air to reach the surface of the metal, and there will be no more action once the film has formed. Pure aluminum, though, is not strong enough for aircraft structure and it must be alloyed with other metals to get the required strength. Figure 6-1 shows the metals used as alloying agents.

Any time we have an alloy, there is the possibility of getting dissimilar metal corrosion, and the surface of the metal must be protected. The aluminum alloy skin of an airplane may be protected from corrosion, and at the same time made attractive in appearance, by a coating of pure aluminum. This is called cladding. In the manufacture of clad aluminum, pure aluminum is rolled onto the surface of the alloy. It actually penetrates the alloy and becomes a part of it, accounting for 1.5% to 5% of the total sheet thickness. This cladding is anodic to the core material, and any corrosion that takes place will attack the cladding rather than the core. The oxide film that forms on the cladding is extremely thin, very tight and transparent, and will prevent further corrosive action.

### b. Surface oxide film

The characteristic of aluminum to form an oxide film on its surface, a film that resists further oxidation, is of real value in protecting the aluminum from corrosion. Metallurgists have found ways of forming films on metal surfaces that are hard, decorative, waterproof and air tight. There are two ways in which this film may be formed. It is most generally done in production by an electrolytic process known as anodizing. In the field, it is generally done by a chemical process known as Alodining.

### (1) Electrolytic treatment

In the anodizing process, the part to be treated is cleaned in a hot water bath with a special non-caustic

| ALLOY NUMBER | SILICON | COPPER | MANGANESE | MAGNESIUM | CHROMIUM | ZINC |
|---|---|---|---|---|---|---|
| 1100 | · · · · · · · · · · · · · · · · · · · · · 99.00% PURE ALUMINUM · · · · · · · · · · · · · · · · · · · · · · · · · · · | | | | | |
| 2017 | | 4.0 | 0.50 | 0.50 | | |
| 2024 | | 4.5 | 0.60 | 1.50 | | |
| 2117 | 2.5 | | | 0.30 | | |
| 3003 | | | 1.20 | | | |
| 5052 | | | | 2.50 | 0.25 | |
| 5056 | | | 0.10 | 5.20 | 0.10 | |
| 6061 | 0.60 | 0.25 | | 1.00 | 0.25 | |
| 7075 | | 1.60 | | 2.50 | 0.30 | 5.60 |

*Figure 6-1. Alloying elements commonly used with aluminum.*

soap solution and then made the anode in an electrolytic process. Chromic acid and water form the electrolyte. After the formation of the oxide film, the part is washed in hot water and air dried. Aluminum treated by this process has not been affected appreciably in regard to its tensile strength, its weight or its dimensions. The anodic film on aluminum alloy is normally a light gray color, varying to a darker gray for some of the alloys. Some aluminum alloy parts, such as fluid line fittings, are dyed for identification. This dye is applied in the anodizing process where it colors the oxide.

When the film first forms, it is an aluminum hydroxide which is porous and quite soft. In this condition it can absorb dust. As the film changes into aluminum oxide, it becomes hard and nonabsorbent, and forms the protective film needed to shield the metal from moisture and air, preventing corrosion.

The anodic film on aluminum alloys is an electrical insulator, and must be removed before any electrical connection may be made. Bonding straps are often connected directly to an aluminum alloy part, and for this attachment, the anodizing must be removed by sanding or scraping.

**(2) Chemical treatment**

When small parts are fabricated in the field, or where the protective anodizing film has been damaged or removed, the part may have a protective film applied by chemical rather than electrolytic methods. This process uses a chemical known as Alodine 1201, or if an invisible film is desired, Alodine 1001. These preparations are proprietary products which meet MIL-C-5541 specification. Alodine can be applied to a surface that has had all traces of corrosion mechanically removed. The surface should be cleaned with a metal brightener and cleaner until it will support an unbroken water film. Any breaks in the rinse water film indicate the presence of wax, grease, or oil on the surface, and further cleaning

must be done. While the surface is still wet with rinse water, brush or spray on a liberal coating of the Alodine chemical. Allow it to stand for from two to five minutes, and rinse it off. While the Alodine is working, the surface must be kept wet. If it is allowed to dry, streaks will appear, and the film will not be adequately protective. Only an area of such size that can be kept wet should be worked at any one time. After Alodine has had its full working time, it should be flushed from the surface with a spray of fresh water. If a swab or soft brush is used, care must be taken to not damage the film, which is quite soft while wet. Allow the surface to dry. After it is dry, it is ready to paint. A satisfactory job produces a uniform yellowish-brown iridescent film, or transparent film, depending on the treatment.

If a powder appears on the surface after the material has dried, it is an indication of poor rinsing or failure to keep the surface wet during the time the Alodine was working. If the powder shows up, the part must be re-treated.

*Warning:* Rags or sponges used in the application of the Alodine material must be kept wet, or thoroughly washed out before discarding. Rags drying with the chemical in them can constitute a fire hazard.

**c. Organic film**

One of the most universally used corrosion control devices for metal surfaces is a good coat of paint. On porous surfaces, paint adherence is no large problem; but on some metal surfaces, it may be difficult to get the paint to stick. The surface of aluminum must be prepared in order that the paint will have a rough surface on which to adhere. The surface may be roughened with a mild chromic acid etch, or by either anodizing or Alodining. All of these treatments provide a good base for the primer to which the paint film will adhere. A good mechanical roughening of the surface may be accomplished with a careful sanding using 400 grit sandpaper. When sandpaper is used, it is imperative that every bit of the sanding dust be removed with a rag damp with thinner before applying the primer.

For lacquer and enamel, the primer which has been used for years is zinc chromate. This is an inhibiting type primer, meaning that the film is slightly porous and water can enter it and cause some of the chromate ions to be released and held on the surface of the metal. This ionized surface prevents electrolytic action and inhibits corrosion. Zinc chromate conforms to specifications MIL-P-8585A and may be either a yellow green or a dark green color. It is thinned with two and one half to three parts of toluol,

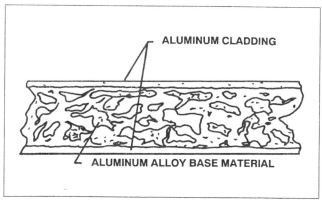

ALUMINUM CLADDING

ALUMINUM ALLOY BASE MATERIAL

*Figure 6-2. Aluminum cladding.*

or some of the proprietary reducers made especially for zinc chromate. The surface to be painted is checked to see that it is absolutely free of finger prints or any traces of oil, and a thin, wet coat of zinc chromate applied with a spray gun. The synthetic resin base of zinc chromate primer provides a good bond between the finish and the metal. It also has the property of being dope proof; that is, aircraft dope will not cause it to lift.

A real boon to the aircraft mechanic has been the availability of zinc chromate in aerosol cans, already mixed and ready to spray. When a repair is made or a part fabricated, it can be given a good coat of zinc chromate and corrosion checked before it ever gets a chance to start.

The newer finishes such as the acrylics and polyurethanes require a wash primer for their adherence. A wash primer is a two part material consisting of a resin and an alcohol-phosphoric acid catalyst. To use a wash primer, the surface is thoroughly cleaned and the primer mixed. Allow the primer to stand for thirty minutes before spraying. The primer is sprayed on with a light tack coat and then a full bodied, wet coat. The primer should be allowed to dry for at least four hours and the top or finish coat should be applied within 46 hours.

Because of the complexity of these new finishes, before attempting to paint an airplane using such a material, you must consult and follow the paint manufacturer's recommendations in detail.

## C. Treatment of Ferrous Metals

### 1. Mechanical corrosion removal

Unlike aluminum, the oxide film that forms on ferrous metals is porous and will attract moisture and continue to convert the metal into corrosion or rust. All traces of this rust must be removed. The most effective method of removing it is by mechanical means. Abrasive papers, wire brushes, both hand and power driven, may be used, but the most effective way of getting all of the corrosion products from unplated steel parts is by abrasive blasting. This gets to the bottom of the corrosion pits. Sand, aluminum oxide, or glass beads may be used effectively. If a part has been plated, either with cadmium or chromium, care must be taken to protect the plating, as it is usually impossible to restore it in the field.

Highly stressed steel parts such as found in landing gears must be cleaned with extreme care. If corrosion is found on these parts, it should be removed immediately by removing the absolute minimum amount of material. A fine stone, fine abrasive paper, or pumice may be used. Wire brushes should not be used as they cause minute scratches which promote stress concentrations and potentially weaken the part. If abrasive blasting is used, it must be done with caution, using only very small grit abrasive or glass beads.

After all of the corrosion has been removed, the rough edges of any pits or damage must be faired with a fine stone or 400 grit abrasive paper, and the surface primed as soon as possible. A dry, clean surface is an ideal setting for new corrosion, and if not protected immediately will allow new damage to begin. Zinc chromate primer may be used on most freshly cleaned steel surfaces.

### 2. Surface treatment

#### a. Plating

#### (1) Nickel or chrome plating

This electroplated coating of nickel or chromium is used to form an air tight coating over the metal to exclude air and moisture from the base metal. There are two types of chrome plating used in aircraft maintenance. Decorative chrome is used primarily for its appearance and surface protection, but hard chrome is used for wear resistance on piston rods, cylinder walls, and other parts subject to abrasion. Parts using hard chrome are normally ground undersize, and plated to the proper dimensions. Engine cylinder walls are normally plated with a porous

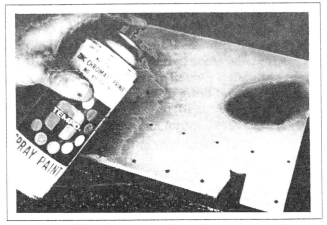

*Figure 6-3. Zinc chromate primer forms a corrosion-inhibiting film on the surface of the metal.*

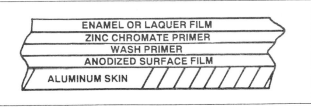

*Figure 6-4. Build-up of finished system.*

24

chrome whose surface has thousands of tiny cracks which hold lubrication.

### (2) Cadmium plating

While chrome plating protects steel by excluding moisture from its surface, cadmium plating protects it in an entirely different way, by sacrificial corrosion. In Figure 1-1 we see that cadmium is below steel in the electro-chemical series. This means that if these two metals are involved in an electrolytic action, corrosion will take place and' the anodic material, the cadmium, will be corroded, while the cathodic material, steel, will not be damaged.

Almost all steel aircraft hardware is cadmium plated. This soft silvery-gray metal is electroplated on the steel parts to a minimum thickness of 0.005 inch. It provides an attractive finish as well as protection against corrosion. When the cadmium plating on a part is scratched through to the steel, galvanic action takes place in which the cadmium corrodes. If the steel should corrode, action could continue until the part is ruined, but the oxides which form on the surface of cadmium are similar to those which form on aluminum; that is they are dense, airtight and watertight. No further action can take place once the initial film has formed. This type of protection is known as sacrificial corrosion.

### b. Galvanizing

Some steel parts such as fire walls are treated with a coating of zinc. The protection afforded by galvanizing is similar to that provided by cadmium plating: it is sacrificial corrosion. When scratched through, zinc will corrode and provide an airtight oxide film. The zinc is applied by passing the steel sheets through vats of molten zinc, then rolling them through a series of rollers.

### c. Metal spraying

Aircraft engine cylinders are sometimes protected from corrosion by spraying molten aluminum on their surface. The steel cylinder barrel is sandblasted absolutely clean and dry. Aluminum wire is fed into an acetylene flame, and high-pressure compressed air blows the molten aluminum onto the surface. Corrosion protection afforded by this treatment is sacrificial corrosion, such as is provided by cadmium or zinc coatings.

## 3. Organic coating

Since paint is an effective and widely used corrosion protection system, its film must not be allowed to break down. The surface to be painted must be properly prepared. Dry abrasive blasting will remove all surface oxides and roughen the surface enough to provide a good bond for the paint. Parts which

have been cadmium plated normally must have their surface etched with a five percent solution of chromic acid before the primer will adhere. After a clean, dry surface has been prepared, a thin, wet coat of zinc chromate primer is sprayed on and allowed to dry. The final finish can usually be applied after about an hour.

# D. Treatment of Magnesium Alloys

## 1. Mechanical corrosion removal

Magnesium is one of the most active of the commonly used metals for aircraft construction, but its weight to strength ratio is such that designers will accept its corrosiveness. A magnesium alloy does not naturally form a protective film on its surface the way aluminum does, so special care must be taken that the chemically or electrolytically deposited film is not destroyed.

Magnesium corrosion occupies a larger volume than the pure metal so it will raise the paint, or if it forms between skins will swell the joints. When corrosion is found on a magnesium structure, all traces must be removed and the surface treated to inhibit further corrosion. Since magnesium is anodic to almost all of the commonly used aircraft structural metals, the removal of corrosion cannot be done with metallic tools. They will leave contaminants imbedded in the metal and cause further damage. Stiff nonmetallic brushes or nylon scrubbers may be used to remove corrosion from the surface or from pits. Deep pits must be cut out with sharp steel or carbide tipped cutting tools or scrapers. Carborundum wheels or paper must not be used because of its tendency to contaminate the surface and cause galvanic corrosion.

If abrasive blasting is used, use only glass beads which have been used for nothing but magnesium. Scale left in the abrasive from other metals can be imbedded in the magnesium and further damage occur.

## 2. Surface treatment

After all of the corrosion possible has been removed from the surface, a chromic acid pickling solution which conforms to MIL-M-3171A Type 1 (Dow No. 1) should be applied to neutralize any corrosion products left. A satisfactory substitute solution may be made by adding about fifty drops of battery acid (sulfuric acid) to a gallon of ten per cent chromic acid solution. Apply this to the surface with rags and let it stay for about ten or fifteen minutes; then rinse thoroughly with hot water. A treatment which forms a more protective film is a dichromate conversion treatment, Dow No. 7, which conforms to MIL-M-3171A Type IV. This solution is applied to the metal and allowed to stand until an oxide film of golden brown appears uniformly on the surface. Rinse with cold water and dry with an air blast. The oxide film is very soft when wet and must be protected from excessive wiping or touching until it dries and hardens. This film is continuous and protects the magnesium surface from corrosion by excluding electrolyte from the surface.

Like aluminum alloys, magnesium can also have a film deposited on the surface by electrolytic methods. Anodizing magnesium by the Dow No. 17 process produces a hard, surface oxide film which provides a good base for further protection with a paint finish.

Magnesium is such an active metal, and magnesium skins are usually so thin, that it is absolutely vital that only the proper solutions and proper procedures be used for corrosion treatment. For this reason, rather than mixing your own pickling and conversion coating solutions, it is recommended that prepared chemicals meeting the appropriate MIL specifications be used, and that the manufacturer's procedures be followed in detail.

## E. Assessment of Corrosion Damage

Removal of the corrosion products and the formation of an inhibitive film on the surface will stop further damage being done to an aircraft structure. But after this action has been taken, the structure must be carefully examined to determine that these repairs have left sufficient material for the required strength.

All pits which have been ground out should have their edges feathered to leave a clean shallow depression at least twenty times the depth of the cleaned out area. If there are several pits close together, they should be blended into one smooth repair, without any surface irregularities or waviness. Extra fine sand paper should be used for the final sanding and the depression polished with fine rouge or pumice to get rid of any scratches that would either cause stress concentrations or hold moisture.

Extreme care must be taken when removing corrosion products from internal areas where there are stiffeners. These areas are usually difficult to reach, and as a result it is easy to grind into the stiffener, or to form a pocket between the stiffener and the skin where new corrosion can form.

Especially difficult in this regard is the structure used in integral fuel tanks where all joints and seams

Figure 6-5. *Remove the minimum amount of material that will get rid of all of the corrosion.*

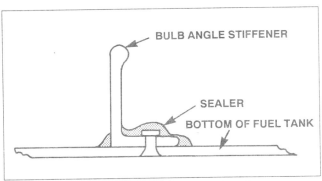

Figure 6-6. *Sealer used in integral fuel tanks.*

are covered with sealing compounds. Corrosion may form under the sealer. If it does, every bit of the compound must be removed to get to the corrosion. There is no substitute for patience and care when working in these areas.

After all of the rework has been finished, the depth of the cleaned out area, or the amount of material left should be determined by using a dial indicator or an ultrasonic tester on the thicker skins or castings. The manufacturer should be consulted if there is any question regarding the strength of the repaired structure. For thin skins, any damage in a critical area which has caused the removal of an appreciable percentage of skin thickness would be cause for replacement of the affected skin.

# Study Questions

1. What type of cleaner can be used to remove all of the dirt, grime and exhaust residue from an aircraft structure?

2. Who should an airplane be placed in some location out of the direct sun when washing it?

3. What can be used to remove stubborn stains from an aircraft?

4. Who is it important that all of the corrosion products be removed from an aircraft structure as soon as they are discovered?

5. How can you be sure that the paint remover you are using will not damage the aircraft structure?

6. How does paint remover actually remove paint?

7. What must be done if paint remover is splashed on the skin or in the eye?

8. What can be used to remove mild corrosion from the surface of an airplane?

9. What type of brush can be used to remove corrosion deposits from an aluminum structure?

10. How can severe corrosion be removed from an aluminum structure?

11. What can be done when removing severe corrosion to be sure that the ends of all intergranular cracks have been cleaned out?

12. What can be used to neutralize any remaining corrosion after mechanical cleaning?

13. How does cladding protect aluminum alloys from corrosion?

14. How does anodizing protect an aluminum alloy structure from corrosion?

15. How is an anodized film deposited on a piece of aluminum alloy?

16. Is an anodized film hard or soft?

17. Is an anodized film an electrical conductor or is it an insulator?

18. What is the appearance of a satisfactory Alodine treated surface?

19. What should be indicated by the appearance of a powder on a surface that has just dried after Alodine treatment?

20. How does zinc chromate primer protect the surface from corrosion?

21. What type thinner is used with zinc chromate?

22. What must be done to a clad aluminum surface to give zinc chromate better adhesion?

23. What is a wash primer?

24. What must be done to a wash primer before it is ready to spray on a surface?

25. What type of cleaning is best for removing all of the corrosion products from rusted steel parts?

26. Why should wire brush cleaning not be used on highly stressed steel parts?

27. How does chrome plating protect a steel part from corrosion?

28. How does cadmium plating protect a steel part from corrosion?

29. What metal is used for the protective film in galvanizing?

30. What must usually be done to a cadmium plated part for paint to stick to its surface?

31. Will natural magnesium oxide protect a surface from further oxidation or corrosion?

32. Who is magnesium more corrosive than aluminum?

33. What type of tools may be used to remove corrosion from magnesium skin?

34. What precaution should be observed when using glass bead blasting to remove corrosion from a magnesium surface?

35. What can be used to neutralize any corrosion which could not be mechanically removed from a piece of magnesium?

36. How does a magnesium conversion coating protect the surface?

37. How can you be assured that the chemical treatment for magnesium is of the proper strength and composition?

38. Name two methods of determining the thickness of a skin after removal or corrosion damage.

39. What should be done to a thin skin that has been extensively damaged by corrosion?

# Chapter VII

# Corrosion Control — A Summary

To summarize any book on corrosion, we can safely say that we do not prevent corrosion; we only control it by eliminating one or more of the basic requirements for its formation:

1. We can prevent the electrical potential difference within the metal.
2. We can insulate the conductive path between areas of potential difference.
3. We can eliminate any electrolyte which could form a conductive path on the surface of the metal. Certain basic operations will accomplish this.

## A. Cleanliness

A clean, polished surface cannot provide a place for corrosion to start. Dirt, grease accumulation, or partially broken paint film can hold an electrolyte in contact with the surface of the metal and promote corrosion.

Airplanes should be kept clean and waxed. A good emulsion-type cleaner will remove dirt film and industrial contaminants which serve to attract moisture to the surface. It is especially important that the inside of the airplane be kept clean, with particular attention paid to the areas where moisture can collect. All drain openings must be kept clean. Deposits which have formed from the engine exhausts must be removed before they cake on the surface and cause the formation of corrosion.

## B. Corrosion Inhibiting Films

Ferrous metals are susceptible to corrosion damage because they form porous oxides. This allows moisture and oxygen to enter and be held in contact with the base metal so corrosion can continue. To prevent this, a coating of metal which forms a continuous or non-porous oxide film is plated or sprayed onto the surface of the steel. Cadmium or zinc are both less noble than steel and will be the one to corrode when the two are in contact with an electrolyte. The oxides of both of these metals are non-porous and prevent oxygen from reaching the steel, thus protecting it.

Aluminum alloys corrode easily because of the electrode potential difference between the alloying agents and the aluminum. Fe aluminum combines with oxygen in the air to form a non-porous oxide film which excludes oxygen and moisture from the base metal and prevents further action. In order to get the strength of an alloy with the corrosion resistance of pure aluminum, a thin coating of pure aluminum is rolled onto the surface of the alloy. If the slight loss of strength caused by cladding is not desirable, unclad aluminum alloy may be protected by an electrolytically deposited or a chemically formed nonporous oxide film. This anodize or Alodine film, in addition to protecting the metal, forms a good base for paint.

Magnesium alloys are protected in the same way as aluminum by the use of a non-porous film either produced by an electrolytic process or by a chemically produced oxide film. Corrosion forms at points where the film has been disrupted, as at rivet holes, skin edges, or scratches in the surface. A good protective coating of paint is vital for the exclusion of oxygen or moisture from the surface.

## C. Dissimilar Metal Insulation

It is often required that different metals be held in contact with each other. When this is the case, dissimilar metal, or galvanic, corrosion can take place. In order to minimize this danger, some form of insulation must be provided.

### 1. Fasteners

When steel fasteners are used in an aluminum structure and subjected to a corrosive environment, the holes should be drilled and countersunk, then treated with Alodine and primed with zinc chromate. The bolts or screws should be coated with the primer and installed wet. This treatment does not insure a completely insulated joint installation, but it does exclude moisture from the joint.

### 2. Skin lap joints

In any joint between dissimilar metal skins, special care must be taken to see that there is no good conductive path between the metals. After the skins have been cut to size, fitted and drilled, coat each faying surface with at least one coat of zinc chromate primer. Allow the primer to dry completely between each coat, and attach the skin with rivets wet with zinc chromate. If one of the skins is made of magnesium, at least two coats of zinc chromate should be applied to each surface, and a strip of three mil (0.003 inch thick) pressure sensitive vinyl tape applied between the faying surfaces. If, for reasons of high temperature, or relative motion between the skins, this tape is impractical, an additional couple of coats of zinc chromate primer should be used. Dip the rivets in the zinc chromate and drive them while they are wet.

## D. Sealers and Sealants

The higher speeds reached with modern aircraft have brought out requirements for aerodynamic sealers used to fair the edges of skins on the wing surfaces. Airplanes flying at high altitudes require that the cabins be pressurized, so every place where plumbing or electrical wires pass through a bulkhead, these openings must be sealed with some form of plastic sealer. Integral fuel tanks are actually part of the wing structure where every rivet joint is sealed to prevent fuel leakage.

Electrical connectors are "potted", sealed with a special sealer to prevent water entering the plug and causing the terminal to corrode. This could cause intermittent electrical connections.

All of these sealers have specific requirements and are used for unique operating conditions. When replacing any sealer, be very sure to use the exact same material as originally used, or a substitute specifically approved by the airframe manufacturer. Follow the recommendations of the manufacturer of the sealer in minute detail. These materials are usually of the two component type, having one container of resin and one of accelerator or catalyst. The mixing sequence, proportions, time, and temperature must be rigidly adhered to. Otherwise, there is likely to be an insufficient bond between the sealer and the metal.

When making a repair, every trace of the old sealer must be removed and the surface prepared for the new sealer. Clean the surface with the recommended cleaner and remove every trace of fuel, oil, or fingerprints. Apply the new sealer and feather the edge down exactly as the instructions specify. This type of material is critical and has no tolerance for careless work or non- recommended methods of application.

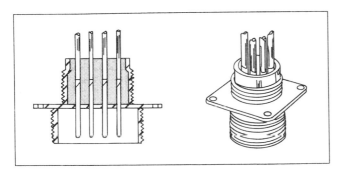

*Figure 7-1. Potted electrical connectors.*

## E. Surface Finishes

The finish applied to modern aircraft serves a purpose more than just being decorative. It forms a protective film which excludes oxygen or moisture from contact with the metal. In this way corrosion is prevented. Metal aircraft may have either an enamel or a lacquer finish.

### 1. Enamel

Enamels are simply pigments mixed into a varnish base. Bases of the older and more simple enamels were resins dissolved in oils. The most popular enamel finishes in use today are polyurethane enamels. These finishes are of the chemically cured, two component type, in which a catalyst is mixed into the resin and the mixture sprayed onto the surface. This type of material produces an exceptionally hard, high gloss finish which resists chalking and weathering. One problem inherent with this type of finish, however, has been the formation of filiform corrosion under the finish. This is minimized by the use of a special filiform corrosion inhibiting primer.

### 2. Lacquer

The pigments used in lacquers are dispersed in a nitrocellulose film along with plasticizers, to give the film a resilience and prevent its cracking. Lacquers do not have the filling characteristics of enamels, and the surface must be more smoothly sanded for the same finish. Lacquers which use acrylic resins are among the popular finishes for modern aircraft because of the durability of the finish. They may be used on steel, aluminum, fiberglass, or magnesium structure.

### 3. Aluminum pigmented finishes

Ultraviolet rays from the sun have a damaging effect on aircraft finishes. Seaplane floats, aircraft wheels and landing gears are subject to hard usage from the atmosphere and from abrasive damage from water and runway debris. To afford the best possible protection to these parts they are usually finished with aluminum pigmented varnish or lacquer.

The aluminum powder differs from ordinary pigments in that, instead of being granular, it is actually composed of tiny polished aluminum flakes. When these flakes are suspended in liquid of the varnish or lacquer, they float to the surface; and because of the surface tension, form a leafed or plated surface which completely covers the material being finished. This overlapping aluminum surface excludes the ultraviolet rays from the sun and protects the finish, thus increasing the life in a very marked way.

## Conclusion

Corrosion is the most damaging natural phenomenon the aviation technician must contend with. The thin, highly reactive metals with which our airplanes are built make them especially vulnerable to its attack. Once corrosion has started on a structure, it opens the way for more, and this continues until the structure is destroyed.

Corrosion cannot be prevented, but it can be controlled, and this is the job of the aviation technician. While corrosion itself is highly complex, its control is mainly a matter of good housekeeping. The structure must be kept clean and dry, and any breaks in the finish repaired immediately. Any corrosion found must be promptly removed and the surface treated to neutralize and residue and inhibit further formation.

Some of the modern surface treatments, sealers, and finishes are complex and will tolerate no improper procedures in their mixing or application. For this reason, it is imperative that the A&P technician understand and follow in detail, specific instructions from the manufacturer of these products.

This IAP training manual is to provide you with a good background for understanding this damaging electrochemical action, and through knowledge help you keep ahead in this battle with the elements.

## Study Questions

1. Why is a perfectly clean surface far less likely to corrode than a dirty surface?

2. How does cadmium plating prevent steel corroding?

3. Why does clad aluminum not corrode as readily as unclad aluminum?

4. What is done to prevent galvanic corrosion between a steel bolt and an aluminum alloy skin?

5. How can corrosion be minimized between an aluminum bracket and a magnesium skin?

6. What instructions must be followed when applying a sealer to an integral fuel tank?

7. What type of cure is used with a polyurethane enamel?

8. What can be done to minimize filiform corrosion under polyurethane enamel?

9. What is the difference between a lacquer and an enamel?

10. How does aluminum lacquer protect a surface from the damaging effect of the sun's rays?

# Glossary

This glossary of terms is to provide a ready reference to the meaning of some of the words with which you may not be familiar. These definitions may differ from those of a standard dictionary, but are in line with standard shop usage.

**abrasive**  A material containing minute particles of some substance which will tend to wear any surface which they rub.

**accelerator**  A chemical added to polyurethane enamels to speed the drying when low temperatures and high humidity conditions are encountered.

**acid**  A chemical substance containing hydrogen, having a characteristically sour taste, and prone to react with a base or alkali to form a salt.

**alkali**  A chemical substance, usually the hydroxide of a metal. It has a characteristically bitter taste, and is prone to react with an acid to form a salt.

**alloying agent**  A metal, other than the base metal in an alloy.

**Alodine**  A registered tradename of Amchem Products, Inc., for a conversion coating chemical which forms a hard, unbroken aluminum oxide film, chemically deposited on a piece of aluminum alloy. Alodining serves the same function as anodizing, but does not require an electrolytic bath. It conforms to specification MIL-C-5541B.

**aluminum alloy**  A physical mixture of metals in which aluminum is the base and other metals are added for specific characteristics.

**amalgamate**  To form an alloy with mercury.

**anode**  The positive plate of an electro-chemical combination, such as a battery or electroplating tank. Electrons leave the anode and travel to the cathode, leaving the anode less negative, or positively charged. When electrons leave an anodic material, the chemical composition of the anode changes from a metal to a salt from reaction with the electrolyte, and the anode is corroded or eaten away.

**anodic**  The component of an electrolytic cell which is positive is said to be anodic because it has supplied electrons for the reaction and is the material that is corroded or eaten away.

**anodizing**  The formation of a hard, unbroken film of aluminum oxide on the surface of an aluminum alloy. This film is electrolytically deposited by using the aluminum as the anode and chromic acid as the electrolyte.

**atom**  The smallest particle of an element that can exist alone or in combination.

**bacteria**  Microscopic plant life that lives in the water entrapped in fuel tanks. The growth of bacteria in jet fuel tanks causes a film which holds water against the aluminum alloy surface.

**battery**  A chemical cell in which electrons are caused to flow from one pole, the anode, to another pole, the cathode, by a chemically produced potential difference.

**bilge**  The lowest part of an aircraft structure where water, dirt, and other debris accumulate.

**biocidal action**  The function of certain fuel additives which kill microbes living in water in aircraft fuel tanks. This prevents scum which would promote corrosion in these tanks.

**black light**  Ultraviolet light whose rays are in the lower end of the visible spectrum. While more or less invisible to the human eye, they excite or make visible certain materials such a fluorescent dyes.

**borescope**  An optical tool with which a visual inspection can be made inside an area where it is impossible to get the eye. It consists of a light, mirrors, and lenses.

**Carborundum**  A trade name for a manufactured aluminum oxide abrasive similar to natural emery. It is used for grinding wheels and for abrasive papers. catalyst A chemical material which is mixed with a polyurethane finish to activate it and begin its chemical curing process.

**cathode**  The negative plate of an electro-chemical combination. Electrons are attracted from the anode to the cathode.

**cathode ray**  oscilloscope An electrical measuring instrument in which the readout is on the surface of a tube similar to that in a television set. Electrons are made to strike the inside of the tube where they cause the coating of the tube to glow. Recurring voltage changes are displayed on this tube in the form of a green line.

**cathodic protection** Another name for sacrificial corrosion (see). A material more anodic than the material being protected is attached to or plated on the material, which then becomes the cathode and is not corroded.

**chemical compound** A substance formed by the chemical reaction between two or more chemical elements.

**chemical element** A fundamental substance that consists of atoms of only one kind.

**chemical salt** The result of the combination of an alkali with an acid. Salts are generally porous and powdery in appearance and are the visible evidence of corrosion in a metal.

**chemical reaction** A chemical alteration in a substance. This is always accomplished by an energy change.

**chromic acid etch** A solution of sodium dichromate, nitric acid, and water. This is used to etch or roughen the surface of a metal to make it better for paint adherence.

**cladding** A method of protecting aluminum alloys from corrosion by rolling a coating of pure aluminum onto the surface of the alloy. This is done in the rolling mill and it reduces the strength of the material somewhat.

**concentration cell corrosion** A type of corrosion in which the electrode potential difference is caused by a difference in ion concentration of the electrolyte instead of a difference in galvanic composition within the metal.

**conductor** A material, usually a metal, which allows a free flow of electrons.

**conversion coating** A chemical solution used to form a dense, non-porous oxide film on the surface of magnesium or aluminum.

**corrosion** An electro-chemical process in which a metal is transformed into chemical compounds which are powdery and have little mechanical strength.

**delaminated** A condition caused by exfoliation corrosion in which the layers of grain structure in an extrusion separate from one another.

**developer (dye check)** A powder sprayed on a surface which has been treated with a penetrating dye. The powder acts as a blotter, pulling penetrant out of any crack, exposing it.

**dye penetrant inspection** An inspection method for surface cracks in which a penetrating dye is allowed to enter any cracks present, and is pulled out of the crack by an absorbent developer. A crack appears as a line on the surface of the developer.

**electro-chemistry** That branch of chemistry which deals with the electrical voltages existing within a substance because of its chemical composition.

**electrode** An electrical conductor, normally one where electrons enter or leave a device.

**electrode potential** A voltage that exists between different metals and alloys because of their chemical composition. It will cause an electrical current to flow between these materials when a conductive path is provided.

**electrolyte** A chemical liquid or gas which will conduct electrical current by releasing ions to unite with ions on the electrodes.

**electrolytic** The action of conducting electrical current through a nonmetallic conductor by the movement of ions.

**electromagnetic radiation** Electrical energy of extremely high frequency and short wave length. This energy will penetrate solid objects and expose photographic film after passing through the object.

**electron** The most basic particle of negative electricity. It spins around the nucleus of an atom, and under certain conditions can be caused to move from one atom to another. Electrons that travel in this manner are called free electrons.

**electro-plating** An electro-chemical method of depositing a film of metal on some object. The object to be plated is the cathode, the metal which will be deposited, the anode, and the electrolyte is some material which will form ions of the plating metal.

**empennage** The tail surfaces of an airplane.

**emulsion-type cleaner** A chemical cleaner which mixes with water or petroleum solvent to form an emulsion (a mixture which will separate if allowed to stand). It is used to loosen dirt, soot, or oxide films from the surface of an aircraft.

**enamel** Pigments dispersed in a varnish base. The finish cures by chemical changes within the base.

**entrained water** Water held in suspension in aircraft fuel. It is in such tiny droplets that it passes through filters and will do no damage until the temperature of the fuel drops to the point that these tiny particles accumulate or coalesce to form free water in the tank.

**exfoliation corrosion**   A form of intergranular corrosion that attacks extruded metals along their layer-like grain structure.

**fairing**   Shaping the contour of an uneven repair so as to form a smooth contoured depression.

**faying surface**   An overlapping surface.

**ferrous metal**   Iron, or any alloy containing iron.

**fiber optics**   An optical inspection procedure which uses a tool composed of tiny glass rods which conduct light and vision. The flexibility of a bundle of fiber rods makes inspection around corners practicable.

**filiform corrosion**   A thread- or filament-like corrosion which forms on aluminum skins beneath polyurethane enamel.

**fluorescent**   A substance is said to be fluorescent when it will glow or fluoresce when excited with ultraviolet light. Some types of dye penetrant material use fluorescent dyes which are pulled from the cracks by a developer and observed under "black" ultraviolet light.

**flux**   A material used to cover the pool of molten metal in the process of welding. The flux excludes oxygen from the weld by forming oxides which remain on the surface.

**fretting corrosion**   Corrosion damage between close fitting parts which are allowed to rub together. The rubbing prevents the formation of protective oxide films and allows the metals to corrode.

**galvanic action**   Electrical pressure within a substance which causes electron flow because of the difference of electrode potential within the material.

**galvanic grouping**   An arrangement of metals in a series according to their electrode potential difference.

**galvanizing**   The application of a coating of zinc on steel by dipping the steel in a vat of molten zinc.

**hydrocarbon**   An organic chemical compound containing only hydrogen and carbon. This is the common type of fuel for both jet and reciprocating aircraft engines.

**inhibitive film**   A film of material on the surface of a metal which inhibits or retards the formation of corrosion. It does this by producing an ionized surface which will not allow the formation of corrosive salts on the metal.

**integral fuel tank**   A fuel tank of an aircraft formed by closing off a section of the structure into a fuel-tight container.

**interference fit**   A fit between two parts in which the part being put into a hole is larger than the hole itself. In order to fit them together, the hole is expanded by heating, and the part is shrunk by chilling. Then, when the two parts reach the same temperature they will not separate. The area around the hole is subject to tensile stress and thus vulnerable to stress corrosion.

**intergranular corrosion**   The formation of corrosion along the grain boundaries within the metal alloy.

**ion**   A charged atom. That is, one with either more electrons than protons (negative ion), or more protons than electrons (positive ion).

**kilovolt**   One thousand volts.

**lacquer**   Pigments dissolved in a volatile base in which the cure is effected by the evaporation of the solvents.

**laminar**   Layer-like; arranged in layers.

**lay of a control cable**   The twist of the strands of a wire cable.

**litmus paper**   An indicator paper which will change color when it comes in contact with an acid or an alkali. It turns red when wet with an acid, and blue with an alkali.

**megahertz**   One million cycles per second.

**mercury trap**   A container in the pick-up tube of a vacuum cleaner used to retrieve spilled mercury. The mercury is sucked up by the cleaner and deposited in the bottle, which prevents it being sprayed out by the discharge of the cleaner.

**metal**   A chemical possessing most of these characteristics: usually rather heavy, with a bright and shining surface, malleable, ductile, and a good electrical conductor.

**metallic ion concentration cell corrosion**   Corrosion that results from a concentration of metallic ions in the electrolyte. The area of high concentration of metallic ions is the cathode.

**microbes**   Microscopic forms of animal and plant life. They exist in water and feed on hydrocarbon aircraft fuel. Microbes form a water-entrapping scum on the bottom of jet aircraft fuel tanks.

**mixture**   A combination of matter composed of two or more components not bearing fixed proportions to one another. No chemical action takes place.

**molecule**   The smallest particle of an element or compound that is capable of retaining its chemical identity of the substance in mass.

**neutron**   An electrically neutral portion of the nucleus of an atom.

**noble (nobility)**   Chemically inert or inactive, especially toward oxygen.

**nucleus**   The center of an atom consisting of protons and neutrons.

**oxidation**   A chemical action in which a metallic element is united with oxygen. Electrons are removed from the metal in this process.

**oxide film**   A layer or coating of metallic oxide on the surface of a material.

**oxygen cell corrosion**   A type of corrosion that results from a deficiency of oxygen in the electrolyte.

**piano hinge**   A continuous metal hinge consisting of hinge bodies attached to both the fixed and movable surfaces. A hard steel wire connects the two bodies and serves as the hinge pin.

**pickling**   The treatment of a metal surface by an acid to remove surface contamination.

**pitting**   The formation of pockets of corrosion products on the surface of a metal.

**plasticizer**   A chemical used in a lacquer finish to give the film its flexibility and resilience.

**polyurethane enamel**   A two-component, chemically cured enamel finishing system, noted for its hard, flexible, high-gloss finish.

**porous chrome**   A plating of hard chromium on bearing surfaces. The surface of the plating consists of tiny cracks in which lubricant can adhere to reduce sliding friction.

**potential**   A term for electrical pressure or voltage caused by dissimilar metals in an acid solution or an electrolyte.

**precipitate**   To condense out of or separate from a mixture.

**proprietary reducers**   Thinners or solvents for paints which are formulated according to and distributed under a trade name of a chemical manufacturer.

**proton**   The positively charged portion of an atom. This makes up part of the nucleus.

**pulse-echo method of ultrasonic inspection**   A method of detecting material thickness or indications of internal damage by introducing a pulse of ultrasonic energy into a part and timing its travel through the material and back to the point of injection.

**pumice**   An extremely fine natural abrasive powder used for polishing metal surfaces.

**quenching**   Rapid cooling of a metal as part of the heat treating process. The metal is removed from the furnace and submerged in a liquid such as water, oil, or brine.

**relief tube**   An installed urinal that drains overboard. The discharge area around these tubes is an area highly susceptible to corrosion.

**resonance method of ultrasonic inspection**   A method of detecting material thickness or indications of internal damage by injecting variable-frequency ultrasonic energy into a material. A specific frequency of energy will produce the greatest return in a given thickness of material. When the equipment is calibrated for a specific thickness, and this thickness changes, an aural or visual indication is given.

**resonant frequency**   The frequency of a source of vibration that is exactly the same as the natural vibration frequency of the structure.

**resonate**   A mechanical system is said to resonate when its natural vibration frequency is exactly the same as the frequency of the force applied. When an object resonates at a particular frequency, the amplitude in its vibration will increase immensely as that frequency is reached, and will be less on either side of that frequency.

**sacrificial corrosion**   (See cathodic protection.) A method of corrosion protection in which a surface is plated with a metal less noble than itself. Any corrosion will attack the plating rather than the base metal.

**seam welding**   A method of electrical resistance welding which forms a continuous line of weld instead of individual spots. (See spot welding.)

**solution**   A state in which a base metal and alloying agents are united to form a single, solid metal.

**spot welding**   A form of electrical resistance welding in which current is passed through sheets of metal stacked together. The electrodes which carry the current into the metal force the sheets together. When the metal between the electrodes melts, it forms a button of metal, joining the sheets.

**stiffener**   A structural member attached to an aircraft skin for the purpose of making it more stiff. It is quite often an extruded angle or a formed hat section.

**stress corrosion**  Corrosion of the intergranular type that forms within metals subject to tensile stresses which tend to separate the grain boundaries.

**sump**  A low area in a fuel tank in which water will normally collect.

**tensile stress**  A stress which tends to pull a material apart.

**transducer**  An electrical device that either takes electrical energy and changes it into mechanical movement, or mechanical movement and changes it into electrical energy.

**ultrasonic inspection**  A method of nondestructive testing using high-frequency mechanical energy.

**uniform surface corrosion**  A general covering of corrosion in which the action has been even. No pits or localized damage have formed.

**viscosity**  The property of a fluid that resists internal flow; the "stickiness" of a fluid.

**volt (voltage)**  A measure of electrical potential or pressure.

**wash primer**  A self-etching primer used in aluminum or magnesium. It is often used to prepare the surface for zinc chromate primer.

**X-ray**  An electromagnetic radiation of extremely short wavelength, capable of penetrating solid objects and exposing photographic film.

# Answers to Study Questions

## Chapter I

1. An atom is the basic unit of a chemical element, and a molecule, made up of atoms, is the basic unit of a chemical compound.

2. A charged, or unbalanced, atom.

3. Corrosion, a salt of aluminum.

4. The metal is converted into a chemical salt.

5. A voltage difference that exists within metal alloy because of the chemical characteristics of the different metals.

6. Copper.

7. Aluminum.

8.
   a. There must be an area of unequal electrode potential.
   b. There must be a conductive path through the metal between these areas.
   c. A conductive, chemical path must join these areas on the surface.

9. Eliminate one of the three basic requirements.

## Chapter II

1. Corrosion formed by a gaseous rather than liquid electrolyte.

2. Iron oxide will continue to grow at a rather uniform rate once it has started. Aluminum oxide will form fast at first, but almost stop once the film has formed.

3. Exclude the presence of any electrolyte from the surface by the use of an oil or grease film, or paint.

4. Corrosion pits.

5. A clump of white powder on the surface.

6. It allows the grain structure within the metal to grow to such a see that there are appreciable anodic and cathodic areas.

7. Small blisters will appear on the surface of the metal.

8. Ultrasonic or X-ray.

9. Replacement of the part.

10. Extruded sections.

11. The aluminum.

12. Low oxygen concentration.

13. Tensile stress.

14. No.

15. Remove and replace them.

## Chapter III

1. Water that accumulates on concrete floors will absorb enough lime from the cement to form an alkaline solution which will corrode the aluminum.

2. Mercury very rapidly forms compounds with aluminum and breaks it down into corrosion products, or salts.

3. Rinse it thoroughly with fresh water each time it is taken out of the salt water.

4. Microbes and the water in which they live.

5. It holds water against the aluminum alloy structure.

6. It kills the microbes, preventing the formation of the scum.

## Chapter IV

1. Exhaust gases contain the products necessary to form an electrolyte with the water which condenses on the surface.

2.
   a. Cracks and seams.
   b. Areas under the fairings.
   c. Under the hinges and fasteners.

3. An acid- or alkaline-proof finish, depending on the type of battery in use.

4. Bicarbonate of soda and water.

5. Boric acid and water.

6. Sump jars hold the agents which neutralize battery fumes.

7. It will hold water against the structure and cause corrosion.

8. The water the litmus paper tested is acidic.

9.
   a. Chemicals from the runway and water form a potent electrolyte.
   b. Abrasive damage from water, dirt and debris thrown up into the wheel wells during takeoff and landing.

10.
   a. In anti-skid sensors.
   b. Under bolt head or nuts.
   c. Under marking tape on tubing.

11. The spot welding process may have left an enlarged grain structure.

12. Look for waviness of the skin along the line of spots.

13. Keep the hinge lubricated with a water-displacing, thin-film lubricant.

14. A thin-film, water-displacing lubricant.

15. To prevent the accumulation of water in the bilge areas.

16. Keep the area clean and protected with a film of water-displacing lubricant.

17. They normally carry a large amount of direct current electricity which accelerates the formation of galvanic corrosion.

18. The tube is filled with hot linseed oil, drained, and the hole plugged with a drive screw or sheet metal screw.

19. Relieve the tension on the cable, open it by twisting against the lay, and look between the strands.

20. Water displacing lubricant spray.

21. Scrub with hot water and a stiff-bristle brush.

22. Coated with a transparent plastic film that excludes all moisture and air.

## Chapter V

1. The technician's eyes.

2. a. Clean the area thoroughly and spray on the penetrant.
   b. Allow it to penetrate and wipe off all excess from the surface.
   c. Spray on developer and examine for signs of the penetrant on the developer.

3. Cracks may be so full of corrosion products that they will not allow any penetrant to seep in.

4. Yes.

5. a. Pulse-echo method.
   b. Resonance method.

6. a. False indication can disguise a fault.
   b. Elaborate equipment and special training are required for complete inspection.

7. Dark.

8. Radiation monitor badges are worn and developed after an exposure time to show the amount of radiation the wearer has received.

9. The voltage applied to the tube.

10. Low power.

## Chapter VI

1. Emulsion-type cleaners.

2. So the surface will not dry before the cleaner has had an opportunity to loosen the surface dirt.

3. Emulsion cleaner mixed with varsol or kerosine.

4. Corrosion will continue to convert the metal to salts as long as any of it is allowed to remain on the surface.

5. Try it on a similar piece of material.

6. It causes the finish to swell and break the bond with the surface.

7. Flood the eye with fresh water and get medical aid as soon as possible.

8. Nylon scrubbers and a non-chlorinated household cleanser.

9. Nonmetallic bristle or aluminum wire brush.

10. Abrasive blasting with glass beads.

11. Grind out all of the crack and then just a little more metal.

12. Treat it with chromic acid or Alodine.

13. It prevents the electrolyte coming into contact with the dissimilar metal of the alloy.

14. It forms a hard, non-porous oxide film on the surface to exclude air and moisture from the surface.

15. Electrolytically. The part is the anode, and chromic acid is the electrolyte.

16. Soft when it is first formed, but it hardens as it ages.

17. Insulator.

18. A uniform, iridescent yellowish-brown finish.

19. Either the surface was not kept wet, or it was not properly rinsed.

20. Chromate ions are held on the surface of the metal.

21. Toluol.

22. Etched with a mild chromic acid etch or roughened with fine sandpaper.

23. A self-etching primer using an alcohol-phosphoric acid catalyst to do the etching.

24. It should be mixed and allowed to stand for 30 minutes before spraying.

25. Abrasive blasting.

26. The scratches could cause stress concentrations.

27. It excludes moisture and oxygen from the surface.

28. By sacrificial corrosion.

29. Zinc.

30. Etched with chromic acid.

31. No.

32. It is chemically more active than aluminum and will react with almost all of the commonly used structural metals.

33. Sharp steel or carbide tipped cutting tools.

34. Do not use glass beads which have been used on any other metal.

35. A chromic acid pickling solution.

36. It forms a hard, non-porous oxide film on the surface of the metal.

37. Use material prepared especially for the type treatment you are using.

38. Dial indicator or ultrasonic tester.

39. Replace it.

## Chapter VII

1. Dirty surfaces hold electrolyte in contact with the metal.

2. Sacrificial corroding. The cadmium becomes the anode and is corroded instead of the steel.

3. The pure aluminum on the surface forms a continuous, non-porous oxide film to exclude air and moisture from the base metal.

4. Insulate the hole with zinc chromate and install the bolt wet with zinc chromate.

5. Generally coat both the skin and the bracket with zinc chromate primer and insulate the two pieces of metal with vinyl tape.

6. The recommendations of the manufacturer.

7. Chemical.

8. Use a special filiform-inhibiting primer.

9. Enamel cures by a chemical action in the resins. Lacquer dries by the evaporation of solvents.

10. Aluminum powder is in the form of tiny flakes. They form a light-tight film over the surface and exclude the damaging rays of the sun from the surface.

# Aircraft Corrosion Control
# Final Examination

Place a circle around the letter for the correct answer in each of the following questions.

1. **How does cladding protect an aluminum alloy surface from corrosion?**
   A. Prevents oxygen reaching the alloy.
   B. Provides a surface that is cathodic to the alloy core.
   C. Provides a good base for paint.
   D. Does not protect the alloy. It is only for appearance.

2. **What type of inspection would be least effective for intergranular corrosion?**
   A. X-Ray
   B. Ultrasonic
   C. Dye Penetrant
   D. Visual

3. **What action may be taken to protect jet aircraft integral fuel tanks from corrosion due to microbial growth within the tank?**
   A. A biocidal additive is used in the fuel.
   B. The entire inside of the tank is painted with zinc chromate.
   C. Rubber liners are installed in the tanks.
   D. Large containers of potassium dichromate crystals are used to ionize the water that accumulates in the tanks.

4. **Where would stress corrosion most likely form?**
   A. On the top skin of an aircraft wing.
   B. In the area surrounding a bolt hole.
   C. In an aluminum casting in which a tapered pipe fitting is installed.
   D. In a skin which has a compressive stress imposed on it.

5. **What should be done to a control cable having some internal corrosion?**
   A. Remove the corrosion and paint it with zinc chromate.
   B. Spray the corrosion with a water displacing lubricant film.
   C. Coat the cable with Par-al-ketone.
   D. Replace the cable.

6. **What should be done to the flux on the surface of the metal, after welding aluminum?**
   A. Remove all of the flux by abrasive blasting.
   B. Remove all flux by scrubbing with a fiber bristle brush and hot water.
   C. Paint over the flux with zinc chromate primer.
   D. Flux should never be used when welding aluminum.

7. **How does cadmium plating protect a steel part?**
   A. Cadmium is less corrosive than the steel and will not corrode.
   B. Cadmium provides a good base for zinc chromate which actually does the protecting.
   C. Cadmium excludes moisture and oxygen from the surface of the steel.
   D. Cadmium is more corrosive than steel so it forms the anode and is the metal corroded. The steel is protected.

8. **What is a conversion coating for aluminum or magnesium?**
   A. A surface treatment which forms a continuous oxide film on the surface of the metal.
   B. A coating of an organic film which protects the surface from air or moisture.
   C. An electrolytically deposited film such as anodizing.
   D. A soft, highly porous film which provides a bond for the primer.

9. **Which statement is true regarding zinc chromate and wash primer?**
   A. Zinc chromate primer does not etch the surface.
   B. A wash primer does not etch the surface.
   C. Both primers are of the two component type.
   D. Zinc chromate primer must never be used over a wash primer.

10. **How does zinc chromate primer protect a surface?**
    A. Forms an air-tight seal over the surface.
    B. Releases chromate ions which inhibit the formation of corrosion.
    C. Prevents any electrolyte from reaching the metal surface.
    D. Does not protect the surface, but serves only as a good base for further paint finishes.

11. **What is the purpose of the developer in a dye penetrant inspection?**

   A. It is drawn to the crack by electrostatic attraction.

   B. It seeps into the crack and makes it show up.

   C. It glows under a "black light" to show up any crack.

   D. It acts as a blotter to draw out any penetrant that has seeped into a crack.

12. **How does an aluminum pigmented lacquer protect a surface?**

   A. It forms an anodic surface to protect by sacrificial corrosion.

   B. It excludes air and moisture from the surface.

   C. It prevents the sun's rays from destroying the lacquer film.

   D. It forms a good, tight bond between the metal and the zinc chromate primer.

13. **Which statement is true regarding iron oxide and aluminum oxide?**

   A. Both are formed by a reaction between the metal and oxygen.

   B. Both continue to grow at a fairly uniform rate once they start.

   C. Both are damaging to the metal and must be completely removed in the process of corrosion control.

   D. Both form a porous film on the surface of the metal.

14. **How can improper heat treatment cause intergranular corrosion?**

   A. The grains within the alloy are enlarged and form more effective anodic and cathodic areas.

   B. The metal becomes more porous and will allow electrolyte to get into the grain structure.

   C. The surface becomes so rough that the electrolyte remains in contact with the metal.

   D. The metal is changed so that all of the anodic area is on the surface.

15. **What may be done to protect the inside of a welded steel tube engine mount from corrosion?**

   A. The tube is cadmium plated, inside and out.

   B. The tube is filled with zinc chromate and welded shut.

   C. The tube is filled with linseed oil, drained, and the hole plugged with a metal screw.

   D. Welded steel tube engine mounts are made of stainless steel and will not corrode.

16. **What is usually the best repair for a part in which intergranular corrosion is found?**

   A. Soak the part in a water-displacing, thin-film lubricant.

   B. Remove the corrosion by mechanical means and paint the surface with zinc chromate.

   C. Replace the part.

   D. Remove the corrosion and re-anodize the part.

17. **Which statement is true with regard to X-Ray inspection?**

   A. X-ray is especially adapted to uniform surface-type corrosion.

   B. High power X-rays are the type best adapted to corrosion detection.

   C. An area of corrosion damage will ap pear on an X-ray negative as a dark area.

   D. Corrosion damage can be detected with little special training and experience, once the film has been exposed.

18. **How are electronic printed circuit boards protected from corrosion?**

   A. By painting them with a conversion coating.

   B. By completely coating them with a transparent plastic film coating.

   C. By using the principle of sacrificial corrosion.

   D. Anodizing the board before installing it in the equipment.

19. **What type cleaner is recommended for removing stubborn exhaust stains from the nacelle behind the engine?**

   A. Emulsion cleaner mixed with water.

   B. Emulsion cleaner mixed with varsol.

   C. Emulsion cleaner mixed with chromic acid.

   D. Toluol and lacquer thinner.

20. **What could be used to remove corrosion from magnesium parts?**

   A. Carborundum paper with grit no larger than 400.

   B. Clean glass beads.

   C. An aluminum wire brush.

   D. Chlorinated household cleanser.

# Aircraft Corrosion Control
# Answers to Final Examination

| | |
|---|---|
| 1. A | 11. D |
| 2. D | 12. C |
| 3. A | 13. A |
| 4. C | 14. A |
| 5. D | 15. C |
| 6. B | 16. C |
| 7. D | 17. C |
| 8. A | 18. B |
| 9. A | 19. B |
| 10. B | 20. B |